A Treasury of
Adoption
Miracles

A Treasury of
Adoption
Miracles

True Stories of God's Presence Today

Karen Kingsbury

WARNER
Faith®

NEW YORK   BOSTON   NASHVILLE

Scriptures noted NIV are taken from the HOLY BIBLE: NEW INTERNATIONAL VERSION®. Copyright © 1973, 1978, 1984 by International Bible Society. Used by permission of Zondervan Publishing House. All rights reserved.

Warner Faith
Time Warner Book Group
1271 Avenue of the Americas, New York, NY 10020
Visit our Web site at www.twbookmark.com.

The Warner Faith name and logo are registered trademarks of the Time Warner Book Group.

Printed in the United States of America

First Warner Faith Edition: April 2005
10 9 8 7 6 5 4 3 2 1

Library of Congress Cataloging-in-Publication Data
Kingsbury, Karen.
    A treasury of adoption miracles : true stories of God's presence today / Karen Kingsbury.
        p. cm.
    ISBN 0-446-53337-8
    1. Adoption—Religious aspects—Christianity. 2. Adoption—Case studies. I. Title.
    HV875.26.K55 2005
    248.8'45—dc22   2004026382

Book design by Charles Sutherland

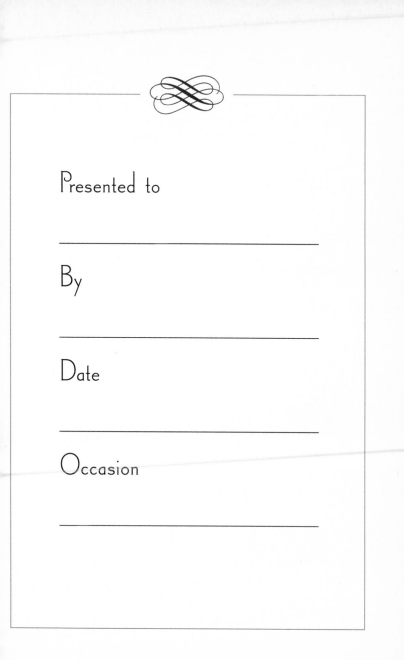

Presented to

_____

By

_____

Date

_____

Occasion

_____

Dedicated to . . .

Everyone who has ever prayed for, cared for, or given love to an adopted child. May God continue to lead you in ways that will allow you to be his heart and hands here on earth. And may every orphan in our midst one day know the love of a family.

And to God Almighty, the Author of life, who grants us wisdom, strength, and ability beyond our own.

CONTENTS

CONTENTS

INTRODUCTION

Adoption is a miracle all by itself.

As I followed up on adoption stories that had come my way over the years, I was struck by that one truth: Every adoption is a miracle. After all, it is God working things out so that a hurting orphan finds his or her way into a family with open arms. It is the building of families in a way that allows God's plans to play out in a very real way.

A special verse in the book of James tells us: "Religion that God our Father accepts as pure and faultless is this: to look after orphans and widows in their distress" (1:27 NIV). That doesn't always mean adoption is right for you. Perhaps that verse means you might pray for a hurting child. Maybe you could support a child internationally—many groups offer the opportunity to send a dollar or more a day to help an orphan eat or receive an education.

But sometimes that Scripture leads people to adoption.

That was the case for our family. As many of you know, we adopted three little boys from Haiti back in 2001. To date, I can tell you that things are going very well. It feels as if Sean, Josh, and EJ have always been with us. They are beautiful, talented children who have a growing faith and are loving to our biological kids. Our story is the last one in this book, so you can read about our miracles there.

I'm best known for my Life-Changing Fiction™, and because of that I receive hundreds of letters each week. Readers often will share their own miracle stories in the process of writing to me. Many of those became the source for the stories you're about to read.

During the research phase of this book, I checked to see what other collections were available. I expected there to be many and was surprised at what I found instead. There are no other collections, at the time of this printing, that detail stories of adoptions in a way that might encourage others to be excited about adoption.

For that reason, it's my prayer that this book will be an encouragement to you. Perhaps you're considering adoption, and this collection will help you make up your mind. Or maybe you know a friend or relative who is considering adoption. Maybe a story in this book will give them encouragement.

But more than that, you probably know someone who has adopted and needs a lift to their spirits. As much as adoption is miraculous, it is also very difficult. It requires adjustments and sometimes a blending of two different cultures—even if the child is an infant. Many times adopted kids have special needs. For those families, and for all who have treaded the waters of adoption, this collection is meant to be an inspiration.

No matter what struggles you're going through,

no matter how many highs and lows, the truth is that adoption is God's handiwork. It is a blessing, a calling, an absolutely divine doing. Dive into the following pages and let God show you again the miracle of a child and the special miracle of adoption.

Don't forget to look for his fingerprints along the way. As much as they're in this story, they're in every adoption that has been or ever will be.

In his light,

Karen Kingsbury

PS: Check out my Web site at www.KarenKingsbury.com to learn more about my adoption story or the Red Gloves series of Christmas novellas or any of my other fiction titles.

A Treasury of

Adoption
Miracles

CHAPTER ONE

A Prayer Each Day

Cindy Henning was only sixteen when she got the news.

The youngest daughter in a family where faith was everything, Cindy had been dating an older boy, someone her parents had warned her about. Though the boy had earned a bad reputation, he had promised things would be different with Cindy.

"We'll kiss, nothing more," he'd told her.

But six weeks earlier things had gotten out of

hand. Now the boy had returned to college across the country, and Cindy was left with the shattering news. Just into her junior year of high school, she was pregnant.

A phone call to the boy proved useless.

"Get an abortion." His tone was clipped, the warmth gone. "Otherwise, don't call me again."

Cindy never did.

Instead, she had trouble eating and sleeping until she was four months pregnant. Then one night she made up her mind. She would keep the baby, drop out of school, and take correspondence courses at home. The life inside her was a child, her very own. Though adoption was a beautiful option for many people, Cindy couldn't imagine giving her baby to someone else.

Finally, well into her fifth month and unable to hide the truth any longer, she told her parents.

"You did the right thing," her father said as he put his arm around her. "Abortion would have scarred you forever."

"Right." Her mother's eyes were soft. "Now we need to find the right family for the baby."

Cindy's heart skipped a beat. "The right family?" She took a step back. "I'm keeping the baby. I already decided."

Her parents exchanged a look. "Honey"—her father lowered his brow—"you're not old enough to be a mother. You haven't learned how to take care of yourself, let alone a baby."

"It's not your decision." Tears blurred Cindy's vision, her voice loud and frightened. "I'm not giving my baby up."

Her mother took a step toward Cindy. "You will do what we say." She brushed a stray piece of hair off Cindy's forehead. "One day you'll thank us."

Cindy fought with her parents the rest of the weekend, but nothing she said changed their minds. Monday night she took a walk around her neighborhood and realized her situation. She was too young to move out on her own, too young to care for herself and a child. Without her parents' support, she could do nothing but follow their orders.

Halfway around the block the realization was clear as water. The baby growing inside her would never be her own. She would give birth, then hand her child to another woman, someone who would raise her child and offer the type of upbringing Cindy could not. The truth caused her to stop in her tracks and lean against the nearest tree. Arms wrapped around her tight midsection, she let the tears come. Waves of them.

That's when she uttered the only prayer she could muster.

"I don't want this, God. Please, whatever happens to my baby, help us find our way back together."

A week later her parents sent her to live with friends three states away. The months passed quickly and Cindy spent most days by herself, reading or taking walks, intimately aware of her baby's movements and sleep patterns. By her seven-month appointment the doctor confirmed what she had already guessed. The baby was a girl.

Cindy was tempted to name her, but she didn't. No use making the loss harder than it had to be. Instead, she called her daughter Baby Girl and often talked to her, sang to her. Prayed over her.

Although the days leading up to her delivery ran together, every moment of her daughter's birth happened in a strange sort of slow motion, the images sharp, pressing themselves into her mind in a way she would remember forever. March 13, 1983, a day Cindy would mark as long as she drew breath.

Some discussion had taken place about whether or not she should hold her baby.

"It'll only make the good-bye sadder," one of the nurses told her. The woman was black with a narrow frame and eyes that glowed even in the dimly lit hospital room.

Cindy hadn't been sure what she would do. But when the moment came, when her daughter was born and after her first cries filled Cindy's senses, the answer was obvious. Of course she would hold her baby girl. She would hold her until someone came and took her away.

The nurse cleaned her up and wrapped her in a white blanket, then she turned to Cindy. "Well . . ."

Cindy didn't say a word because she couldn't. Instead, she held out her arms and nodded. The nurse crossed the room and gave the baby to her. Then, for the sweetest minutes she'd ever known, she cradled her child to her chest, looking at her, seeing past her eyes to the toddler and little girl and teenager her baby would one day become. A sensation swept over her, something she hadn't known before, and Cindy breathed it in.

So this was the feeling mothers everywhere understood. A sense that all time could stop, but life would go on as long as her precious daughter could stay that way forever, cradled in her arms.

Their time together was over almost as soon as it began. The adoption was closed, so Cindy wouldn't meet her baby's new mother. Still, the process was clear. The woman and her husband—a wonderful couple from everything the social worker had said—were waiting in a room down the hall, waiting for the moment when Cindy's baby would be theirs.

States had different laws about such things, but where Cindy lived, she would lose all rights to the baby as soon as the infant went home from the hospital with her new adopted parents. The social worker entered the room and gave Cindy a sad smile.

"How are you?"

Cindy wanted to scream at the woman, tell her to leave them alone because it hadn't been enough time, not nearly enough. She wanted to run with her baby down the stairs, out the front door of the hospital and far away where no one could find them. Instead, she swallowed hard and looked at her baby. The infant's eyes were open, and maybe it was Cindy's imagination but they seemed to be calling out to her, asking her the question that would haunt her all her days.

Why? Why would you give me away? Why didn't you fight harder to keep me?

"Cindy?" The social worker came a few steps closer. "It's time."

Cindy closed her eyes and drew in the faint sweet smell of her daughter, the warm weight of her against her chest. It wasn't the social worker's fault. This was part of the process—she'd been warned. If she chose to hold her daughter, the visit couldn't be long. Otherwise the risk was high that Cindy might change her mind.

She would have two days still, forty-eight hours

when she could refuse the adoption, cancel the whole thing. After that, her daughter would go home with her new family. But if the social worker let her linger in this moment, the outcome would be marred by the emotions of new motherhood.

The social worker came closer still, and Cindy opened her eyes. Then, without drawing out the process another minute, she kissed her daughter's cheek, nuzzled her face, and whispered. "I love you, Baby Girl." Then she looked at the woman and out came the greatest lie she'd ever spoken: "I'm ready."

The ache was immediate and constant.

Long after Cindy returned home and found her way back into the stream of high school classes and football games, way past the days when people talked about her in hushed tones, wondering where she'd been, Cindy missed her daughter with an intensity that frightened her.

Five years later she fell in love with a business major, a man who built houses in the summer for extra money. The man was everything her first boyfriend hadn't been—honest, faithful, and driven to make a life for himself through both integrity and character. Cindy fell hard for him, and two years later they married.

From the beginning she told him about the child she'd given up and how badly she wanted to meet her someday.

"If it means that much to you, I'll pray about it." Her husband crooked his finger and used it to lift her chin a few inches. "Believe, Cindy. One day you'll find her if that's God's plan."

The years went by and Cindy and her husband had three daughters—each one a bittersweet reminder of all Cindy had lost with her first child. She and her parents reconciled, though Cindy could never quite forget what they'd done or how they'd thought it would work out for the best. Though her husband continued to pray for a miracle reunion, the adoption paperwork remained closed, and any time Cindy pursued the subject she was told the same thing.

Finding her daughter would be all but impossible.

More time passed and still Cindy never stopped believing that somehow, someway, God would answer her prayer. She marked the birthdays of the daughter she'd given up and, based on what she knew of her other three, tried to imagine how she might look, what she might be involved in.

One afternoon after a morning in which her first-born girl was heavy on her heart, Cindy showered and headed for school. It was parent-teacher conference day, and she needed to meet with Mrs. Barnett, her youngest daughter's fifth-grade teacher. The meeting was halfway over when Mrs. Barnett paused.

"Oh, I didn't tell you." She smiled. "We have a new student teacher at the school. She'll be with us the rest of the year."

Cindy returned her attention to the notebook of her daughter's writing samples sitting on the desk between them. "That's nice."

"She'll be joining us in a minute. It's part of her training."

There were a million things left to do that afternoon, so Cindy was more concerned that the conference move along so she could be on her way. But at that moment the classroom door opened and a beautiful young woman walked in. Cindy looked at her, and everything seemed to freeze.

The teacher was making introductions, but Cindy couldn't hear them. She stood slowly, her eyes locked on the young woman's. Everything about her was as familiar as the mirror, as familiar as the faces around her dinner table each night. The resemblance was so strong it blocked all sense of propriety or logic.

Cindy said the only thing she could think to say: "Were you . . . were you adopted?"

The subtle confusion in the young woman's eyes cleared instantly. Her mouth hung open for a few seconds and slowly, in a way that told Cindy she wasn't alone in thinking the possibility existed, she nodded. "Yes. I was born March 13, 1983."

March 13, 1983?

A cry came from Cindy's mouth and she brought her fingers to her lips. "I think . . . I think you're my daughter."

The young woman didn't speak. Certainty shone in her expression and rather than compare notes, she came to Cindy and the two fell into each other's arms. It was an embrace that erased the years in a single moment, one that convinced Cindy she was on holy ground because this was a miracle like no other.

"Baby Girl," Cindy whispered into her daughter's soft brown hair. "I prayed for you every day."

Mrs. Barnett was still in the room but she was silent, undoubtedly swept up in the drama unfolding before her.

The young woman drew back and looked at Cindy. "I'm Anna." Tears glistened in her eyes. "And I've had the most wonderful life." She smiled even as two tears fell to her cheeks. "I've prayed for this, too. So that I could thank you in person for what you did."

"Thank me?" All these years Cindy had dreamed of this moment and dreaded it at the same time, certain her daughter would say the thing she had seemed to say as a newborn. *Why?* Why had Cindy given her up? Instead, she was thanking her, and the miracle suddenly became bigger than Cindy could take in.

The conference forgotten, Cindy and Anna

caught up on the twenty-two years they'd been apart. They compared notes to be absolutely certain of their relationship, and there was no doubt. Anna was her daughter, the one she'd prayed for. She explained that she had been raised by a loving family in which she had two sisters and a brother, a family that had given her far more than Cindy could have as a young single mother. Her family was aware that Anna wanted to meet her birth mother one day, and they, too, had prayed for the chance.

Anna took Cindy's hand. "I always believed that somehow we'd meet. Because I was afraid you might've regretted giving me up." She looked deeper into Cindy's eyes. "And I never wanted that. Not when God allowed me the greatest life with my adopted parents."

Cindy held her daughter again and allowed herself to cry, not for the years she'd lost, but for the perfect way God had worked everything out. Her parents had been wrong in many ways, wrong to not acknowledge her feelings, wrong to not listen more to her wishes. But in the long run, they'd been right.

And now she and Anna had come full circle.

"Can I ask you something?" Anna stepped back, her face full of a love that could be described only as complete.

"Yes." Cindy couldn't stop looking at her, marveling at the way she'd known the moment Anna walked into the room that she was her daughter. "Ask anything."

"Could you and your family come this Sunday for dinner?" Anna paused, a grin tugging at the corners of her mouth. "I'd like to meet my other sisters."

With that another certainty grew from the springtime soil in Cindy's heart. The certainty that for the rest of time, she would never again wonder about her daughter or where she was or how her life was going. Because forever more she would be a part of her life.

And that was the greatest miracle of all.

CHAPTER TWO

Brought Together by a Miracle

Angie Wilcox had one purpose, one passion—to help lonely children find families. For that reason, she loved everything about her job as a social worker in Manhattan. She worked in an office not far from the often troubled Hell's Kitchen area and every week brought new girls and boys into her life, kids desperate for a family—either through foster care or adoption.

Her coworkers were, for the most part, as driven

as Angie, as caught up in the welfare of the children in their care. But Angie's reason was personal. She was adopted as an infant, placed into a warm, loving family with six other children. From the time she was very young, she viewed adoption the way it had always been described to her—the most beautiful gift an adult could ever possibly give to a child.

Yet, there were days when New York City was too busy, too confining, days when she dreamed of living in the country and working with kids there. Her personal life was going nowhere in Manhattan. She'd dated an investment broker for three years, but he'd broken things off late that summer and now that it was fall, the coming holidays figured to be lonely.

Still, she had made a commitment to stay in New York. Her caseload was full, the files complicated. Miss Angie, the kids called her, and with everything they had they depended on her. She would stay until God showed her otherwise, because the kids in her borough needed her too badly.

One day that fall, Angie arrived at work and found her supervisor talking with someone in the waiting area. With them was a beautiful girl, brown eyes and curly dark brown hair. Angie guessed at her age. Two maybe, three at the most. The child looked up at her and immediately lowered her chin, too shy to make eye contact.

The adults were still talking, so Angie moved closer to the child and dropped slowly to her knees. "Hi."

At first the girl wouldn't look up. But after a few seconds, she lifted her eyes, brought her fingers up, and gave the smallest wave. Angie felt something in her heart soar. She loved this part, connecting with a child who was probably at the lowest point of her life—alone and without anyone to care for her.

"What's your name, sweetie?" Angie spoke in a whisper, careful to not interrupt the adult conversation going on a few feet away.

The little girl blinked, her eyes huge, fear still casting shadows over her expression. She opened her mouth and then swallowed. Finally she found the courage to say, "Karli."

"Karli? That's a beautiful name." Angie uttered a

silent prayer for the girl. She didn't look ragged and run down the way most kids looked when they first came to social services. Abused and abandoned kids had a certain look in their eyes, a layered look of hurt and hopelessness. Little Karli had none of that.

"Angie . . ." Her supervisor broke the moment.

She stood and smiled. "Another file?"

"Yes." The supervisor was a woman who'd been with the department nearly twenty years. She frowned and motioned for Angie to follow her. "She and her parents were in a car accident last night. Hit by a wrong-way drunk driver." The woman bit her lip. "She was in a car seat—no injuries. Both her parents died. She was brought here from the hospital."

Angie felt her heart sink. "Relatives?"

"None so far. I need you to run a check." She hesitated, her tone soft. "Make it a priority, okay?"

"Definitely." Angie nodded. "How old is she?"

"She'll be three on December 25."

Another wave of sorrow washed over Angie. "Merry Christmas."

"Yep." The supervisor handed her a file. "The information's here. It's all we have, but I think it's enough to run a check." She glanced back at the child. "She doesn't understand what's happened."

Angie nodded. Of course the little girl wouldn't understand, not if she was only two years old. By her next birthday, her parents would be nothing more than a dim memory. The truth was sobering, but it also left hope. If a relative existed, someone who loved the child, then her life would still have promise. She could be adopted and never feel the devastation of this awful time except in the knowledge of it.

She stepped away and headed back for little Karli. This was the best and hardest part of her job—working with children whose lives were hanging in limbo. The child was watching her, looking to her for answers to questions that had to be swarming in her head.

Where were her mommy and daddy? What had happened the night before, when their car got hit? And how come she wasn't home having the type of morning she was used to? Why was she here in this strange office?

Angie breathed another prayer. That God would use her to bring hope and a new family to this precious child. She approached the girl and stooped down again. "Karli, come here, honey."

The child blinked twice, then held out her hand. As she came forward, Angie was seized by the strangest thought. What if she could take Karli for herself, take her home and be the mother she would need? The idea faded as quickly as it had come. Of course that couldn't happen. Angie had promised herself when she took a job in this field that she wouldn't get personally involved. There were too many needy children for her to be distracted that way.

And for three straight years, from the time she'd taken the job as a twenty-three-year-old straight out of college, Angie had kept her promise to herself. But for some reason the child before her seemed different; something about her had found an immediate pathway to the center of Angie's heart.

Karli held out her hand, and Angie wrapped her fingers in the girl's. They walked to Angie's office, and Angie set her up with a doll and some toys in the corner. As soon as Karli was situated, Angie went to work. It took less than an hour to learn Karli's situation.

She had one living relative—a single aunt named Amy who lived outside Denver. Karli called the woman and found out more. Amy was twenty-six and engaged. Her deceased sister had been eight years older, and the two had never been close. They hadn't talked in years, and Amy didn't know until that phone call that she even had a niece.

"I'm all she has?" Shock sounded in Amy's voice. "Is that what you're saying?"

"Yes." Angie sorted through the paperwork on her desk. "I've checked every other angle." She hesitated. "I'd like to bring Karli for a visit. If you're interested, I think it would be better for her than setting her up with strangers."

The young woman on the other end was silent for a moment. "Definitely. You can come anytime, but I can't . . . I can't promise you I'll take her. This is all . . . it's all so sudden. I have to talk to my fiancé."

"Of course." Angie checked her schedule. "I'd like to bring her to see you this weekend. We could be there just after lunch Saturday, if that works for you."

"Okay." Uncertainty rang in her voice, but at least she was cooperating. Amy gave Angie directions and the conversation ended.

As Angie replaced the receiver on the base, she felt a strange nervousness, a trembling deep inside. Amy hadn't heard from her New York sister in years? She hadn't even known about Karli? From the sounds of it, she wouldn't be heading to Manhattan for the funeral, either. What sort of family would lose touch with each other that way? And how would Amy provide a loving home if family wasn't important to her?

Angie tucked her fears into the back pocket of her conscience and stuck with the mind-set she'd been trained to have. Any time a child could be with a healthy, fit relative, the child would always be better off. That night Karli stayed with her, the way children sometimes did when a solution was at hand, when even short-term foster care simply wasn't necessary.

The next day they shared breakfast and then headed to the airport. By the time they were on the plane, Angie felt a connection with the girl that she normally resisted. Every half hour or so, Karli would look up and say, "I want my mommy."

And Angie would say, "Mommy's not here, honey." It was another part of her training. Don't lie to children, telling them their parents would return when that was clearly impossible. No matter how difficult, she needed to be honest. For a two-year-old, it was enough to say that her mother wasn't there. It was the truth, and she wouldn't have understood the concept of death.

They were almost to Denver when Karli fell asleep. Angie used the time to settle against the seat back and stare out the window at the vast blue. As she'd done often since her phone call with Karli's aunt Amy, Angie prayed.

God, work a miracle for Karli. She's lost so much, at such a young age. And if this Amy woman doesn't want her, let it be clear. She paused and waited. Sometimes when she prayed, she felt the Lord's presence very close. As near as her next breath. This was one of those times. She narrowed her eyes. *I feel some-thing special for this one. So if Amy doesn't want her, let me be a part of Karli's life. Please, God.*

Even as she finished the prayer she felt a strange tingling along her spine. She'd never prayed that way for a child in her care. Whatever it was about Karli, it was different, and Angie had the strangest feeling that God was up to something unusual.

They arrived in Denver just after noon, ate a small lunch, and rented a car. Amy lived twenty minutes north of Denver in a rural area. They pulled into the driveway and Angie looked back at Karli. "Okay, honey. We're here." She was careful to not mention that the woman they were meeting was anyone special. In case things didn't work out.

Karli's eyes welled with tears. "Mommy?"

Angie stifled a cry. "Honey, she's not here." She forced a smile. "I'll be with you, okay?"

Once Karli was out of her car seat they headed for the house. At that moment, the front door opened and a woman stepped outside, took three steps along the path and froze in her tracks.

Angie looked at the woman now just ten yards away, and her head began to spin. She might as well have been looking into a mirror. The woman looked exactly like her, and clearly they both saw the resemblance.

"Are you . . . are you Amy?"

"Yes." Her voice was filled with the same shock Angie was feeling. "You look"—she took another step closer—"exactly like me."

"I was thinking the same thing." Angie held tight to Karli's hand. They looked so much alike the child was almost forgotten in the strangeness of the moment.

Amy shielded her eyes from the afternoon sun. "Were you adopted?"

Angie's feet felt suddenly unsteady, and a trembling started in her knees. "Yes. As a baby."

"Really?" Amy uttered a surprised sound and brought her fingers to her mouth. "Me, too."

Angie was breathless, not sure what to say. She looked down at the child beside her. "This is Karli."

Amy smiled at the girl and patted her head. "Okay, Karli and Angie," she said as she looked up. "Let's go inside and talk."

Over the next hour Angie learned the truth about the unimaginable. She and Amy were indeed born on the same day, in the same town. Their birth mother—a woman neither girl knew—must have had identical twins and given them up to separate families. As soon as they realized the truth, they embraced, caught between laughing and crying.

Karli played nearby as they recounted their lives—their love for summer days; their preference of wearing their dark hair in a short, neat cut; the similar courses they'd taken in college. Even their love of peppermint ice cream.

Finally Angie sat back in her chair and stared at her newfound sister. "I was so worried about you."

"Worried?"

"Yes, that you weren't very family-oriented. Because you and your sister had lost touch."

"That was her. She got into trouble young and left the family. None of us had been in touch with her."

"So you're an aunt." Angie looked at Karli. "Have you thought about that?"

Amy smiled. "Have you?"

"Me?"

"Yes." A bit of laughter slipped from Amy's mouth. It took a few seconds, but suddenly it came together. "If you're her aunt"—she grinned—"I'm her aunt, too. Because adopted families are families all the same. Miracle families."

"Exactly."

The plans came together quickly. Reconnected with the identical twin sister she hadn't known existed, Angie moved to Denver. There she is able to marvel at the miracle of her life and spend as much time with Karli as she wants. As for Karli, she's doing well in her new family, with her new forever mother, Amy.

CHAPTER THREE

Twice the Miracle

Bob and Sarah Williams married with one thought in mind: Children were out of the question. Track stars at the University of Illinois, Bob and Sarah saw life as a continuous athletic event. They moved to the Pacific Northwest and took jobs with Nike. Spare time was spent jogging, playing tennis, and working out.

Because of that, life came to a complete standstill when Sarah returned from the doctor one day, still shocked at the news. Despite their efforts to the contrary, she was pregnant. The first six weeks after finding out the news, Sarah was too sick to make any decisions. Her mother—a woman of strong faith—visited and prayed for her.

"God has a plan for this child, Sarah. Otherwise you wouldn't be pregnant. Don't think of all you've lost because of this; think of all that lies ahead."

Sarah had never prayed much, but faced with serious decisions regarding their future and the future of the child, she had nowhere else to turn. "God," she would cry out between bouts of nausea, "if you're there, make it obvious to us. What're we supposed to do?"

Bob, too, found himself praying. "The way I see it, the fact that Sarah got pregnant is a miracle. Now, God, show us whether we should keep this child."

Within a week, Sarah watched a special on an educational cable channel about the stages of child development in the womb. That night she and Bob limited their options to two: Keep the baby, or put it up for adoption.

Sarah was still mulling over the possibilities when she was falling asleep one night and felt the faintest stirrings in her abdomen. Like butterfly wings against the underneath side of her tummy, the feeling continued for several seconds before Sarah realized what she was feeling. It was her baby!

She leaned over and put her hand on Bob's shoulder. "Wake up, Bob; come on." She raised her voice to a loud whisper. "You won't believe this."

Bob moaned twice and then opened his eyes. After a few seconds he looked at the alarm clock on the nightstand. "It's midnight, honey. Can't it wait?"

"No." Sarah could barely contain her excitement. "I felt it, Bob. I really did."

"Felt what?"

"The baby." She put her hand on her abdomen. "Our baby."

Bob opened his eyes wider than before. "You mean . . . you felt it move?"

"Yes!" She made a squealing sound. "It felt like butterfly wings on the inside of me."

Sarah's excitement carried over into the next day and the next few weeks as the baby's movements grew stronger. Her enthusiasm was contagious, and by the time she was six months pregnant, she and Bob were looking forward to being parents. That week they went to the doctor's office and found out the biggest news of all.

She wasn't carrying one baby. She was carrying two. Twin boys, according to the ultrasound.

Joy and disbelief surrounded Bob and Sarah in the days that followed. Life would be exciting having twin sons, and together they'd love them and raise them and teach them to care about athletics. They marveled that at the beginning of this process, they had thought they might never have children.

All that weekend they shopped, setting up the spare bedroom as a nursery complete with matching cribs and a sports theme. But on Sunday night Sarah was seized by sharp pains in her midsection. She and Bob had been reading up on childbirth and were planning to enroll in a class the following week. False contractions were possible, but this pain was strong enough to take her breath away.

By eleven o'clock that night, Sarah was doubled over. Worse, she had started bleeding. "Bob!" She cried out for him and he found her in the bathroom. "Take me to the hospital now. Something's wrong!"

He helped her to the car and took her to Emanuel Hospital where doctors confirmed Sarah's fears. Indeed, something was very wrong. Her placenta had torn and she was bleeding. Black spots fast-danced in front of her eyes as she struggled to understand the doctor's words. The babies were having some sort of trouble, and surgery was imminent.

The man's words ran together and Sarah looked around for her husband. Before she could find him she felt herself slipping, drifting in a way she was helpless to control.

When Sarah woke up nearly two days later, she didn't have to ask Bob what had happened. Her abdomen was smaller than before, and Bob was crying.

"You're awake!" He stood and came to her side.

She didn't want to ask the question, but she had no choice. Without blinking, with barely any sound coming from her voice, Sarah met his eyes and released the words: "Where are the babies?"

"They're . . ." He hung his head for a moment before finding her eyes again. "They're gone."

The grieving process was worse than anything Sarah could have imagined. She never saw her boys, never got to hold them, but still the loss was devastating. Worse, well-meaning friends would on occasion talk about things working out for the best, that maybe Bob and Sarah weren't meant to have kids after all.

As the months passed Sarah learned another sad truth. Her uterus had been too damaged in the miscarriage; more children would be out of the question. But unlike their friends, they were no longer content to live the remainder of their lives without children. Finally, a year after the loss of their twin boys, they began adoption proceedings.

———

Their plan was to adopt a newborn in the United States, a child whose mother was a teenager, too young to raise a child.

The proceedings went slowly; months were needed for a home study and appointments with a social worker. They took evening courses about children at risk and parental bonding. The nine-month mark came, and still no babies.

About that time, Bob and Sarah began to pray again. After losing their boys they'd stopped, not sure of a God who could let their babies die. Sarah's mother explained it best to them.

"God doesn't make mistakes. He promised us there'd be trouble in this world, and there is. But he still asks us to pray."

From that day on, Bob and Sarah did pray. They asked God to bring them a baby, a child who would fill the hole in their hearts. Then one day they received a call from their social worker.

"I've got a little boy for you."

Sarah's heart soared. However long they'd waited didn't matter. God had heard their prayers and now he was giving them a son, a child to ease the place in her heart where her twins had taken root. "How old is he?"

"Well—" The social worker chuckled. "He's not exactly born yet. But if you can get to the hospital in the next hour, you'll probably be there in time for the delivery."

The woman went on to explain that a runaway had been picked up and spilled her story. She had been in foster care when she'd gotten mixed up with the wrong crowd in their small town. Three months later she was pregnant and desperate for answers. She had lived on the streets until a week earlier when she turned herself in to a police officer. A call to her social worker assured her that they would help her find a loving family to adopt her baby.

Bob and Sarah grabbed a blanket and an infant layette, one they'd purchased back before their babies died. They arrived at the hospital and an hour later a doctor appeared in the waiting room.

"The delivery went beautifully. Mother and babies are doing very well."

Sarah blinked and looked at Bob. "What did he say?"

Bob shifted his gaze to the doctor. "Babies? I'm sorry; maybe you have the wrong couple."

"You're Bob and Sarah Williams, right?" The hint of a grin played on his lips.

"Right, but . . ."

"The mother was very young." He paused. "She didn't know it, but she was carrying twins."

At that instant, the social worker entered the waiting room. There were tears in her eyes. "You're approved for more than one child. The babies are both boys. If you're willing to take them, they'll belong to you."

Twin boys? Sarah's knees shook and she grabbed Bob's elbow to keep from falling. Twin boys who needed a home? She thought about the nursery, the one that had been set up since they'd found out she was carrying twins. It was still the way it had been back then—two cribs, twin dressers, all of it ready for two twin boys.

The social worker uttered a sound that was more laugh than cry. "I've never seen healthy twins come up this suddenly." She shrugged. "It must have been meant to be."

"More than meant to be." Bob's voice was thick with emotion. He put his arm around Sarah and gave her a tender squeeze. "It's the miracle we've been praying for."

And so it was. As they took their twin sons home, Bob and Sarah were convinced that the delay had been part of God's plan. For only he could have arranged for twin baby boys to help fill the emptiness left by the infants they'd lost.

CHAPTER FOUR

❦

God's Ways

Margaret and Bill Jefferson did their grieving in private.

After four miscarriages, they no longer desired to talk about children with their families. They had been married six years and wanted babies desperately. But nothing Margaret or her doctors did seemed to make a difference.

Every evening the couple would take a walk through their hilly North Carolina neighborhood and talk about the possibilities, the losses.

"Funny," Margaret would sometimes say, "everyone else treats us like losing a baby early in pregnancy isn't much worse than breaking an ankle."

It was true. For the most part, their family members didn't seem to know how to react to their miscarriages. But for Margaret and Bill the loss was cavernous. They estimated dates and knew the ages their children would have been if they'd lived.

Finally Bill began praying that Margaret would find a friend, someone who might understand the loss she felt, the desperation to be a mother one day. Not long afterward, Margaret signed up to be part of a fiction-reading book club at her church. She'd tried Bible studies but always wound up in tears, bereft and certain no one could understand the pain she was in.

The book club was different. Fiction was an escape Margaret hadn't considered before. She found a handful of authors who wrote real-life fiction, stories that touched her heart and lifted her spirits, characters that helped keep her eyes on Christ.

At the club's fourth meeting, she sat next to a woman named Joanne. From the beginning she sensed something similar about the woman, and over the break that night she realized what it was. The conversation turned to children and Joanne told Margaret she had two girls.

"But I'll always have four children."

"Four?" Margaret sipped her coffee, thoughtful.

"Yes." Joanne smiled, but a familiar pain shone through. "I miscarried twice. Those are babies I won't meet until heaven. But they were mine all the same."

Margaret could barely speak. Her chin quivered and tears welled in her eyes. "I . . . I know what you mean."

Joanne reached out her hand and squeezed Margaret's fingers. "I thought so." She paused. "I prayed that God would use this book club to help me connect with someone, a friend I might have something in common with."

"That's me." Margaret sniffed and managed a smile. Then she told Joanne about all the babies she'd lost. "Last time I was in, my doctor told me we were running out of options." She raised one shoulder. "We've tried just about everything."

Joanne leaned back in her chair. "What about adoption?"

"Adoption?" The word sounded foreign on her tongue. Margaret had always pictured their babies coming from her and Bill—not from a stranger. She swallowed and an idea hit her. "Is that how you . . . ?"

"Yes." Joanne grinned and a lighthearted chuckle slipped past her lips. "We adopted two sisters, girls who wouldn't have had a chance otherwise."

Margaret set down her coffee cup. Adoption had crossed her mind before, but one thing always stopped her from even voicing the idea. "How can you . . . how do you love them like your own?"

"They are my own." Joanne's smile faded some, but a new sort of kindness filled her eyes. "None of our kids really belong to us. If God puts a child in our lives, in our homes, then that child is our own for as long as God desires." A sparkle lit up her eyes. "They're all on loan, when you think about it."

Margaret let the idea sink in. All children belonging to God. His to give, his to take, on loan for a season—however long or brief. That night she shared the conversation with Bill. "I met a friend." She curled up next to him on the sofa. "Honey, what do you think about adoption?"

Bill looked at her, his eyes soft. He brushed a lock of hair off her forehead. "I've thought about it."

"You have?" Margaret sat up a little straighter. "You've never said anything about it."

"No." He looked out the window at the shadows that fell across their front yard. "I guess I've been afraid."

Margaret felt her heart go out to him. This was a side of him she hadn't seen before. "Afraid of what?"

He drew a slow breath. "In fourth grade my teacher spent half the year excited about adopting a little boy." He leaned forward and anchored his elbows on his knees. "After Christmas she came back and she was never the same." He looked at her. "The birth mother changed her mind."

"So the adoption fell through."

"Yes." Bill squinted as if the memory hurt still. "I remember hearing her tell another teacher once that no matter where that little boy went, no matter how his life turned out, she would always feel like he was her own."

The image settled in at the center of Margaret's heart. "How awful."

"Yeah." He exhaled through pursed lips. "I hated seeing her like that, this teacher who had been so happy, so excited for the future." The pain lifted some. "Far as I know she never tried to adopt again."

Margaret considered the story. "That's why you never brought it up? For us, I mean?"

"I guess." Bill stretched and stood. "Even talking about it makes me think about the possibilities. Making a plan, knowing a child is coming who belongs to us, and then having a birth mother change her mind." Bill made a face. "Or worse. Taking a baby home and having the mother change her mind then, after we've already connected with a child."

The idea sounded terrifying to Margaret also. But something about it intrigued her. Certainly birth mothers didn't change their minds often. Something that had happened to Bill's fourth-grade teacher wouldn't happen to them. "God knows what he's doing," she would tell Bill over the next several months whenever the conversation came up. "He knows we couldn't stand that kind of loss. Maybe we should look into it a little more."

Finally the conversations convinced Bill to do just that. They contacted a private adoption attorney, and at the first meeting they shared their fears. "We'd rather wait three years than be connected to a birth mother who would change her mind." Bill's tone was resolute. "We've already lost four babies; we couldn't stand another loss."

The attorney shared his understanding of their feelings. "It's up to me how I match you up. You can be sure the adoption is almost 100 percent risk-free."

Almost 100 percent. The phrase caught on the edges of Margaret's nerves. The fact was, nothing was completely certain. As the process unfolded, she remembered to not hang her hopes on the percentages or the attorney's promises. Rather, she and Bill pinned all their hopes on God. He alone knew what they could tolerate, how much they'd already been through.

Early in the process, Margaret and Bill decided it didn't matter if a healthy girl or boy came first; as long as the birth mother was as certain as possible. Six months after finishing their home study, the couple took a call from their attorney.

"I've found a birth mother, someone I'd like you to look at."

Margaret and Bill were at the attorney's office first thing the next morning. The birth mother was twenty-four, and she'd given up one other child two years earlier. She was on welfare and had little maternal instinct. Her notes in the file explained that she didn't believe in abortion, but she had no interest in being a mother. Life was short; she wanted a career and plenty of years to play the field.

The adoption would be open, something the birth mother had requested. Margaret and Bill were fine with that, believing that a woman who had thought things through to that point would be more likely to stand by her decision. Besides, the woman had already given up one child. The odds, their attorney agreed, were as good as they could get.

Months passed and they learned that the woman

was having a girl. Their attorney had advised them to wait on naming the child. "Since you're very concerned about a birth mother changing her mind, it would be best to wait and bond after everything's final."

But it was impossible to follow the man's advice. Aware that their little girl would be coming home in just five weeks, Margaret and Bill went shopping for a pink layette and a whitewashed crib. They named her Brianna Suzanne, decorated her bedroom, and began counting the days until she could come home and be part of their family.

One week after another passed; everything about the adoption was right on schedule. Margaret and Bill took courses in early child parenting and infant CPR. Finally the call came.

"She's in labor. It might be a long wait, but if you get down to the hospital, you'll have a chance to see your daughter as soon as she's born."

Margaret and Bill finished the phone call and looked at each other. Bill held his arms out and pulled her close. "It's really happening."

A lump filled Margaret's throat. They'd lost four

babies, but they wouldn't lose this one. "God's so good. I knew it would all work out."

Bill nodded and let his eyes wander across the kitchen. "In a few days she'll be home and nothing will ever be the same again." His eyes found hers. "Isn't it amazing?"

"Miraculous."

On the way to the hospital, the two of them went over the attorney's instructions. They could visit with the baby while she was in the hospital and as often as they wanted during the forty-eight-hour period when the birth mother could change her mind.

"It's a technicality," the attorney said. "Better than some states; worse than others. Nothing to worry about."

They arrived at the hospital just after six o'clock that evening, and from the beginning they knew something was wrong. When Margaret and Bill entered the maternity waiting room, their attorney was there, talking with a doctor and the social worker.

The conversation came to a standstill when they

walked into the room. Margaret took hold of Bill's hand as her husband looked from the doctor to the attorney. "What's going on? We . . . we weren't expecting you here."

The attorney cleared his throat and gave a strained look to the doctor and social worker. Then his eyes found first Margaret's, then Bill's. "Follow me; we need to talk."

Her heart pounding in her throat, Margaret could barely feel her feet beneath her. Bill squeezed her hand hard as they walked into the hall. "Is something wrong?" Bill asked the question that was lodged in both their throats.

The attorney looked at the floor for a beat and then lifted his eyes. "There's no easy way to say this." He sighed hard and rubbed the back of his neck. "The birth mother's wavering."

Wavering? Was she dreaming? They'd done everything they could to avoid this moment. It wasn't possible. The woman had already given up one baby, after all. Margaret felt her head spinning. "Wavering?"

Bill leaned against the wall. His face was three

shades paler than before. The impossible had happened, just the way he'd feared, and now he looked drained of all hope. "So it's a done deal? She's changed her mind?"

"Not entirely." The attorney shifted his weight. "Apparently her first baby was a boy. She, well, she never wanted a little boy. And when she found out this baby was a girl, she didn't believe it. But now—now that the baby's on her way—the reality is more clear." He hesitated, the words obviously hard for him, too. "She called for the social worker and said something that makes me concerned."

"What did she say?" The glimmer of possibility remained. Margaret wasn't willing to give up on their daughter yet.

The attorney frowned. "She said all her life she's wanted a daughter."

The words hit like so many bricks, tearing at the image she and Bill had shared just a few hours earlier. The image that one day soon their daughter would be home with them, all of them starting their new life together.

"I wouldn't leave yet." The attorney straightened

and crossed his arms. "Might just be last-minute jitters."

Neither Margaret nor Bill said much for the next two hours. They sat alone in a quiet part of the waiting room, praying sometimes in hushed whispers, sometimes by themselves. Margaret's prayer was simple. *God . . . we can't lose another baby. We just can't. Please . . . bring our little girl home to us. We're asking for a miracle, Lord.*

But three hours later the terrible news they'd been dreading was confirmed. The birth mother was adamant and apologetic. She wanted to keep her baby, more than anything in the world. She asked the social worker to pass on the fact that she was sorry, and the entire ordeal was over that quickly.

Before they left the hospital, their social worker told them it could have been worse. "I know you're upset, and I don't blame you." She touched Margaret's arm. "But at least you didn't hold the baby or meet her. That would have made it harder."

The couple left the hospital in a fog. Margaret wanted to pray but she couldn't, didn't know what she would pray about if she could. She had asked that God bring this baby girl home, and things hadn't worked out. The loss was just as great as every miscarriage—a silent sort of grief and loss—a feeling other people wouldn't understand.

For weeks after losing the baby girl, Margaret thought about the child—little Brianna Suzanne. What sort of life would she have with a mother who was so cavalier toward parenting? And would she be raised with the faith Bill and Margaret would have instilled in her? The questions were so daunting, the loss so great, she had no interest in starting the process over again. She and Bill discussed their options and decided they would shelve the idea of parenting for now. If God didn't want them to raise a child, they couldn't do anything to force the issue.

Slowly they returned to their routines, and most days they didn't even talk about children. But one day three months after losing their little girl, the social worker called.

"I've got another baby girl." The woman's voice was bursting with excitement. "She was born a week ago and apparently there was a mix-up. The family she was headed for had already been given another child. So this baby girl is yours if you're in-terested." The social worker went on to explain that the baby's mother was a single woman who had already waived her rights to the child. No danger of a change in plans. Also, the girl was healthy with curly blonde hair and light blue eyes.

Bill and Margaret could barely speak. They looked at each other and their answer was clear im-mediately. Bill cleared his throat. "Yes." He swal-lowed, clearly choked up. "We're interested. Tell us what to do next."

The following few weeks were like something from a dream. Overnight, Bill and Margaret were the parents of an angel baby, a child they named Brianna Suzanne. God had answered their prayer after all, and not a day went by when the couple didn't see their daughter as a heaven-sent gift.

But they didn't realize the true miracle they'd been given until they took a call from the social worker when Brianna was six months old.

"I have . . . some sad news." The social worker sounded awestruck.

Margaret's heart stuck in her throat. She glanced at the smiling child in her arms and kissed her baby's cheek. "What is it?"

"The child you lost out on? The little girl?" The social worker hesitated. "She had a rare heart condition. She died in her sleep last week."

The news hit Margaret like a baseball bat in the stomach. She sat down, cradling her daughter close to her chest. "I'm sorry. Please . . . tell the mother we'll pray for her."

When the conversation was over, Margaret remembered her prayer. *Please, God . . . we can't lose another child.* She studied her daughter's small features and tried to imagine losing her now, after six months. The loss of that baby would have been more than she and Bill could handle, and God had known that. So he took that little girl from them before they could fall in love with her.

And instead God brought them Brianna Suzanne, a miracle baby in more ways than they had known until that morning.

CHAPTER FIVE

※

The Right Place at
the Right Time

Sam Sturgell became an attorney because he was
fascinated by family law. The child of a broken
family, Sam believed that with God's help, an attorney could wreak miracles and goodness rather than
destruction between a couple and their children.

Every day, Sam prayed that the Lord would use
his talents in the courtroom to bring about his pur-

poses in the lives of the people he worked for. For that reason, he wasn't surprised one afternoon when he took a call from Lucy Manning, an old college friend.

Lucy had been a classmate in law school when she lost interest in the long hours of study. She took a job as a flight attendant and decided to pursue her other love—a love for adventure. In the process, she met a windsurfer in Portland, Oregon, a forty-year-old free spirit with a house on Hood River and a disdain for the establishment. The two fell madly in love and whenever Lucy had a few days she spent them on the Columbian Gorge, learning to surf the whitecapped Columbian River.

Everything was perfect until she wound up pregnant. From the beginning, her boyfriend told her he'd support her. But he wouldn't marry her, and he had no interest in being a father. Lucy considered her options and she and her boyfriend had a heart-to-heart conversation.

"Why don't you give the baby up. What a beautiful gift—giving someone a child."

Lucy had to agree. Yes, the pregnancy would set

her back in her career. She'd need to take time off work to pull it off. But somewhere in the Portland area, there was bound to be a couple desperate for a child. Giving the baby up would be the ultimate gift.

But she had no idea whom to contact, so she looked up Sam Sturgell, her old law school buddy, and explained the situation. Sam was happy to help. He lined up several portfolios of families. Lucy picked a couple in Salem, Oregon, a husband and wife with a five-year-old boy and the inability to have more children. Lucy barely noticed a small line near the bottom of the couple's dossier:

Healthy child only.

Her pregnancy progressed without a hitch, and meanwhile Sam kept praying, kept showing up at work every day with the single goal of helping bring children and parents together.

The week that Lucy was scheduled to deliver, across town in Beaverton, Oregon, Anthony and Amber Aarons were reaching a decision. They had been pursuing a path toward adoption for nearly a year. Their home study was complete, and they'd been approved to bring home a child. They had contacted Sam Sturgell and now they were waiting for a baby. But not just any baby.

The week before, the Aaronses were at a soccer tournament when they were struck by something they saw. Their nephew was playing on a team of eleven-year-olds, and one of the boys on the team had a hand with no fingers.

The couple watched the boy, who was a tough defender, block one goal attempt after another. The boy's family was seated not far from Anthony and Amber. Every time he made a strong move, they were on their feet cheering for him.

Everything about the scene took Anthony Aarons back.

Anthony had been born with a cleft palate, a fairly common birth defect in which the tissue between the nose and the lip doesn't develop properly. Surgery was performed on Anthony when he was seven years old—as soon as his parents had the insurance and ability to pay for their part of the operation. But by then the teasing and strange glances from other kids had taken their toll. Anthony's confidence was almost nonexistent, but it was made worse because of his father.

Like Sam's, Anthony's parents divorced, though not until Anthony was ten years old. After that his father, an international traveler, would visit Anthony and his sister two or three times a year. Once he overheard his father talking to his mother.

"Isn't there something you can do for the boy, another surgery, something?" His voice sounded frustrated.

"Lower your voice, please. Anthony will hear you."

"He won't hear me, he's a kid. He's outside playing." His father let loose a loud breath. "He looks terrible, that's all I'm saying. I hate the idea of him going through life looking like that."

Several other times over the next eight years, Anthony would catch his father studying his upper lip area, the look on his face just short of disgusted. Anthony's only saving grace during that time was the love and acceptance he received from his mother. She took him to church and taught him to believe in the plans God had for his life.

When he graduated with a master's degree in counseling, his mother was the first on her feet to applaud. She had believed in him all along, and now his life would be a wonderful one because of her faith, and in spite of the rejection he'd felt from his father.

Those memories were stronger than they'd been in a decade as Anthony held Amber's hand and watched the little boy playing soccer. The child beamed with confidence, convinced—because of the obvious love from his family—that he could do anything he set his mind to do.

On the way home, Amber looked at Anthony and turned down the radio. "I can't stop thinking about that little boy, the one without fingers on one hand."

"Me either." Anthony tightened his grip on the steering wheel and looked straight ahead at the road. "I feel like God's trying to tell us something."

"Like maybe we're supposed to adopt a child with special needs?"

The question rattled the walls of Anthony's soul. It was exactly what he'd been thinking, though he hadn't wanted to say so. He didn't want to lead Amber down that path if she hadn't been thinking it, too. But now . . .

He grinned. "Is that really what you've been thinking?"

"Yes." She uttered a quick laugh. "I want to be that mother, standing on the sidelines cheering for a child who might not get cheers otherwise." She paused. "A mom like your mother was to you."

That Monday, Anthony called their private adoption attorney, Sam Sturgell. "We've had a change in our plans." Anthony went on to explain about the soccer game and the fingerless child. "We'll probably go through the state." He looked out the window of his office. What child would God send them? The adventure was only beginning. "Most private adoptions deal with healthy kids, right?"

Sam Sturgell tapped his pencil on a file in front of him. "Most of the time. But once in a while God has a miracle up his sleeve, a reason why a couple like you would change your mind about wanting a healthy child." He thought for a moment but couldn't think of a single case where the child about to be born might have a disability. "Let's do this: Go ahead and contact the state. But in the meantime, I'll keep your file on my desk and pray. If there's a reason for all this, my guess is we'll know soon enough."

Anthony and Amber began to pray, also. Somewhere a child was either born or about to be born with a lifelong trial. They begged the Lord to bring them the right little boy or girl, someone whose life they could truly impact.

A few days later, out in Hood River, Lucy Manning went into labor. She called Sam, her tone determined. "This is the moment I've been waiting for. This baby belongs to the couple in Salem. After that I can get on with my life."

Sam took the call the hour the baby was born. It was Lucy, and she was crying. "Sam . . . there's a problem."

He could barely make out her voice. "A problem? Lucy, what is it? I can be there in fifteen minutes— what happened?"

"The baby, he . . ." Her voice cracked and it took

a while for her to regain her composure. "He has something wrong. His lip isn't right, Sam. The doctor called it a cleft palate. I'm not sure what this means, but I'm crushed, Sam. Please . . . pray for us."

Sam's heart ached for Lucy and the baby, and for the couple in Salem. He pulled their file from his drawer and immediately spotted the statement that made his heart sink, the statement that confirmed what he already knew to be true about the adoptive couple. They wanted a healthy baby, nothing else.

A call to the couple made the situation sure. Through tears, the couple stated that they felt ill-equipped to handle the needs of a handicapped child. They would have to pass on Lucy Manning's little boy.

Sam was hanging up the phone when his eyes fell on the file belonging to Anthony and Amber Aarons. Suddenly a series of chills ran down his spine. Of course. The Aaronses had changed their mind only a few days before. Not only would they take a baby with a disability, but they wanted such a child.

God . . . you're putting together a miracle, aren't you? He looked up and grinned as his trembling fingers dialed Amber and Anthony's number. As he was dialing he realized something he hadn't considered before. Anthony had a reason to be familiar with disability. Though a person could barely tell now, it was clear Anthony had also been a victim of a cleft palate.

Anthony answered on the second ring. "Hello?"

"Anthony, it's Sam, your attorney. I think we're on the brink of a miracle here."

On the other end, Anthony wished Amber were home. She was out at the market. He moved to the front of the house and looked for her car. "Okay, Sam, what's up?"

"If you could have a child with any certain type of disability, what would you choose?"

It was a strange question, but Anthony didn't hesitate. "I was born with a cleft palate; you probably know that." He clutched the phone a bit tighter. "I guess I would understand that best."

Sam's words didn't come right away. The lump in his throat was too big to slip words past. When he could finally talk, he said, "Anthony, God's brought a baby into the world that couldn't belong to anyone but you and Amber."

Eight years have passed since then. Amber and Anthony adopted little Randall James. Trials have been a part of the journey—during the surgery to correct Randy's disability, and when other kids have been less than understanding. But Randy has a strong spirit, something instilled in him by his parents' faith and determination. That spirit shows up most on the soccer field where Randy is one of the top defenders, and his parents? The best cheering section of all.

CHAPTER SIX

❧

A Child from Heaven

Ben and Beverly Jameson knew it would take all of their resources to adopt a child, but that didn't matter. With their entire hearts they wanted to be parents, but nothing they had tried through medical means had done anything to help Beverly get pregnant.

They contacted a private adoption attorney and learned that the cost would be approximately twelve thousand dollars—money the couple simply didn't have. Finally it came down to one choice. They contacted their bank and took out a second mortgage on their house.

"This will stretch you to the max," the banker told them. "Unless something changes about your income, we won't be able to loan you any more money for at least five years."

In fact, something *was* going to change regarding their income. It was going to decrease. The couple lived outside Detroit, Michigan, where Ben was a manager at a local supermarket. But Beverly wanted to be a stay-at-home mother. She worked as a teacher's assistant, but once they adopted she planned to quit and spend her days with their baby.

"Don't worry about it," Ben told her. "I'll work two jobs if I have to. I want you home with our baby; that's where you belong."

The process took six months, and one afternoon they took the call they'd been waiting for. A homeless couple had found the wherewithal to contact the Jamesons' attorney and inform him that they wanted to give their baby up for adoption. The family was quickly matched with Ben and Beverly, and three weeks later their son, Eric, came home. A few days later the couple heard from their attorney that the homeless woman had gotten her tubes tied after delivering Eric. He would never have a biological sibling.

No matter what struggles they'd gone through to get to that point, Ben and Beverly were thrilled. Beverly quit her job and became a full-time mother. Eric was the child of their dreams—a dark-haired, half-Hispanic child who loved them from the beginning.

The trouble didn't start until Eric was three years old.

One morning Beverly took him from his bed and noticed bruises along his shinbones. Kid stuff, she figured. Eric was very active. Of course he was bound to bruise, the way he ran around the house, banging into furniture during the times when he and Ben wrestled.

But later that week Beverly spotted bruises on Eric's back and shoulders. That night their son spiked a high temperature, one that didn't break for the next two days no matter what they tried. Finally they took him to see the doctor.

The man frowned as he looked at Eric's bruised torso. "We should run some blood tests."

Within a week they knew without a doubt what was wrong with Eric. He had leukemia. His blood type wasn't listed in the bone marrow donor banks, so his family could pray for just one thing—that somehow someone would enter the registry as a match to Eric—a possibility that carried with it odds of twenty thousand to one.

The wait was terrible.

After praying for a child and exhausting their resources on medical intervention for Beverly to get pregnant, the Jamesons had none of the money needed to hold local blood drives, events that could add hundreds or thousands of names to the national registry.

They met with the pastor of their church one Sunday and explained how dire the situation had become.

"We're out of money, out of options." Tears filled

Ben's eyes. "Even if we could find a match, I'm not sure we could pay for it."

The pastor was touched by their plight. He organized an event with a sister church in Detroit, and in one weekend they raised enough money for the Jamesons to pay their part of the bone marrow transplant. The only problem was an obvious one: They hadn't found anyone to match little Eric's blood and bone marrow type.

There were times during that month when Beverly would dream about ways to help her sick son. She would search out the homeless woman who gave birth to him and ask her if she'd had other children prior to Eric. Siblings had a 50 percent chance of being a match, so that was an option Beverly wanted to hold on to.

But the social worker and the attorney had been honest from the beginning. The woman hadn't had children before Eric; and after having her tubes tied, she certainly wouldn't have more.

Another month passed and Eric seemed to grow stronger. His doctor confirmed that he was in remission but warned that the remission was only temporary. Often when a child with leukemia slips out of remission, his disease is more aggressive, worse than before.

Ben and Beverly kept praying.

Then one day a few weeks later, they took a call that stopped their world. Despite the fact that she'd had her tubes tied, Eric's birth mother had given birth to a little girl a year after Eric was born.

"At first the woman wanted to keep the little girl." The attorney could barely get the words out fast enough. "But her husband has a drug problem. They've been on the streets ever since the child was born. She's two now. The woman is pretty sure she wants to give the girl up, and there's only one place she would want her to be—with you and Ben. That way the kids would be full-blooded siblings. She'll let us know next week."

Beverly called Ben immediately. The two prayed desperately on multiple fronts. First, that if it were God's will, the woman would agree to give up her daughter. Living on the streets couldn't be a good environment for a toddler. Second, if they could bring this little girl home, that her blood would be a perfect match for Eric.

"It seems like too much to ask," Beverly whispered to Ben that night.

"But that's the type of God we have, a God who loves doing the impossible." Ben smoothed Beverly's bangs off her forehead. "Remember that, okay?"

Over the next few days, they survived on faith alone. Eric stayed in remission, but he was pale, thinner than he should have been. With every passing hour it was obvious he would need a bone marrow transplant one day soon.

But while they waited, their pastor and the sister church that helped raise money for the Jamesons all prayed around the clock. Finally the news came— the woman had decided to give up her little girl. Ben and Beverly rejoiced in the addition of a daughter to their family. When their attorney arranged the meeting, the couple was shocked to see how much Eric and his sister looked alike.

The little girl's name was Corinne, and the Jamesons chose to keep her name the same. That way she would have one less adjustment to make. Once she'd been home for a week, they took her in for a checkup and the shots she'd missed out on. That's when the doctor drew the blood to test her prospects as a donor for Eric.

By then, Beverly was convinced that a miracle was at hand. The sister who never should have been had wound up in their home. If they looked that much alike, of course their bone marrow would match. And sure enough, when they received word from their doctor they weren't surprised.

Eric's miracle little sister was indeed a match!

The operation was not a risk for a toddler, so the procedure was arranged and a month later the bone marrow transplant took place. Today, fifteen years later, Eric and Corinne are the best of friends. The miracle of Corinne's life lives on in her brother, and Ben and Beverly are grateful every day for the answered prayers that came their way, the brilliant morning that followed the darkest night of all.

CHAPTER SEVEN

Forgiven All Along

Penny Hathaway had big dreams as a teenager.

She wanted to travel the country, maybe spend a year with her actress aunt in Chicago and a year with a family friend in New York City, before settling down in Los Angeles and attending the University of Southern California as a film major.

The daughter of devout believers, Penny was tired of the same old routine, the one that took place every weekend in the small Arizona town of

Camp Verde where she'd been raised. Friday night football, Saturday chores, Sunday church service and potluck. It was so predictable, Penny thought she'd suffocate if she didn't get out.

"She wants all the wrong things," her father told her mother during Penny's last semester of high school. "It's one thing to seek a college degree or a future in the arts. But that girl has something wild in her eyes. It scares me."

Penny's mother agreed. Their daughter had been attracted to the wrong sort of friends, the wrong boys, ever since she entered high school. If she took that wanderlust with her onto the road, she might make mistakes she'd live with a lifetime.

Her entire senior year, Penny worked at a restaurant, saving her tips and wages toward her trip. The day before she left, her parents finally sat down with her and expressed their concerns.

"God has a plan for your life, Penny. Seek after that, okay, honey?"

Penny resisted the urge to roll her eyes. Her parents were so stuffy, so old-fashioned. Part of living a creative life was the right to express one's passions, right? Wasn't that what she read about in the art books she collected? Her parents' faith was stifling, enough to squeeze the life out of her creativity. But instead of arguing, Penny only nodded and smiled. "I'll look for a good church as soon as I'm set up in Chicago."

The early weeks of Chicago life were everything Penny had dreamed. She found a job at one of the city's five-star steak restaurants and struck up a friendship with her aunt. The woman was a free spirit and away from the apartment most of the time. She had no rules for Penny other than one: If you play around, don't get caught.

"Your mother would never forgive me if something happened to you here." She would wink at Penny. "But I was young once. I know what it feels like to be free of your parents' rules. Just be careful."

Penny agreed and by the second week she'd met a dashing young man, a waiter who had a role in the ensemble at one of the big productions playing in the theater district downtown. His name was

Adrian, and he was handsome and talented. Penny felt herself falling for him overnight.

They took walks on the pier and played at the arcade. He took her to see one of his performances, and afterward he showed her around backstage and introduced her to the cast. Penny couldn't believe her good fortune, how quickly she'd taken up with the musical theater set and how different her life was now that she was on her own.

The night of the performance, Adrian took her back to his apartment and gave her the first taste of champagne she'd ever had. Everything about life felt wonderful in that moment. She had the interest of a wonderful guy, and maybe sometime soon the interest would become real love. It was possible.

When Adrian wanted to sleep with her that night, Penny couldn't think of a single reason why she shouldn't. This was part of her new life, wasn't it? Passion with no rules or restrictions? The sort of passion that would only fuel her creativity and bent for the dramatic.

The pattern between them continued for the

next two months, and one day her aunt pulled her aside. "Adrian seems like a nice young man."

Penny couldn't stop herself from smiling. "He's amazing, everything I used to dream about back in Arizona."

Her aunt raised an eyebrow. "There've been more than a few times when you didn't come home." She paused with a slight shrug of her shoulder. "I hope you're being careful."

Penny assured her aunt she was not being too wild, that she knew what she was doing when it came to her hours and her relationship with Adrian. But deep inside she felt the stirrings of panic. Her period was three weeks late, and Adrian hadn't been calling every day like before. At work one of the girls said she'd seen him with one of the girls from his show, walking the pier and holding hands.

"Is it true?" She pulled Adrian aside the next time they worked together. "Are you seeing someone else?"

His expression went from surprise to an easy

amusement. "You weren't kidding about being new around here, were you?"

Penny blinked, not sure what to say. "I don't care where you're from, when you're, well, you know . . . when you're together like us that means no other people."

Adrian chuckled and framed the side of her face with his fingers. "Sweet Penny, that's church talk coming from you. In my world people explore each other. Sometimes one person at a time, sometimes more. Wherever the spirit leads."

Penny left work early that day, drove back to her aunt's house and lay down on her bed, her emotions in turmoil. What had he said? He liked to explore people? That he lived his life according to where the spirit led?

She looked out the window. If Adrian was being led by spirit, then what spirit? The only true and good Spirit was the one her parents worshiped— the Holy Spirit. And certainly God wouldn't want her having a physical relationship with Adrian. Not outside marriage.

And why was her period late?

The questions kept Penny unsettled through the night. She didn't have to be at work until late the next day, so she drove to a drugstore that morning and bought an early pregnancy test. It took less than ten minutes to learn at least one of the answers. She was pregnant.

Everything her parents and even her aunt had warned her about had happened. She had thrown her parents' faith and morals out the window, and now she was in more trouble than ever before. That night after work she told Adrian the news.

"What?" His smile faded and a scowl knit his brow. "I thought you were using something."

"No." Penny could barely breathe. "I . . . I didn't plan to be . . . to be active this soon."

Adrian's expression relaxed. "Well, little one, I'm sure you'll figure something out."

It was the last time Adrian sought her out for any reason. The few times she tried to make contact with him, he had things he was doing, excuses why he couldn't spend time with her or take her out the way he had before.

Finally, when she was ten weeks pregnant, she told her aunt what had happened.

"Maybe my parents were right." Penny wiped at her tears. Her entire life seemed to be crashing down around her.

"It's not too late to live life their way, Penny." Her aunt put her arm around her shoulders. "Let's figure out a plan to get your life back on track."

Penny was certain about a few things. First, she couldn't let her parents know about her pregnancy. Second, she couldn't keep her baby. She was not yet ready to be a mother. Even if she was finished with living wild, she couldn't care for a child. She still wanted to visit New York City and wind up at USC.

But she couldn't have an abortion, either. Not if she wanted to turn her life around and make better choices. Penny worked until her seventh month and then took time off. She contacted an adoption attorney and explained what she wanted to do. The adoption would be closed, he told her. No contact until the child reached eighteen, and then only if he or she wanted to look into the files.

Penny agreed to the terms, and two months later she gave birth to a healthy baby boy. She held him for just fifteen minutes, awestruck over his perfect features and full head of dark hair. He would be artistic, she figured. Handsome and tall like his father, sensitive and curious like her.

The social worker came then, explaining that the adoptive couple was waiting in a room down the hall. "Everything will be just fine." The woman took her baby and gave a small nod of her head. "The couple is very nice. Your baby will have a wonderful life."

The minute the door closed behind the woman, Penny was struck by a terrible thought. She hadn't said good-bye. She had held her baby and marveled at him and loved him fiercely for the few minutes they had together. But she hadn't said good-bye. And somewhere deep within her heart a seed of guilt took root. How would her son feel about her when he was old enough to realize what she'd done? She'd chosen adventure and college over being a mother to her son.

As soon as the thought formed in her mind, she

knew she was wrong. She had done the very best thing a mother in her situation could do. Giving her baby up for adoption had been much harder than she had ever imagined, but it was the right thing to do, no question.

Still, as the years passed, Penny marked her son's birthdays and Christmastimes, imagining what he might be like at various ages, what his interests might be, and whether he knew about her. Six years later she graduated from USC and came clean to her parents about the baby she'd given up. Her mother was crushed, Penny could see that much. But she agreed with Penny that adoption had been the best choice given the circumstances.

Penny wanted to tell her mother that sometimes, on cool autumn evenings or warm summer nights, she still found herself thinking about him, imagining what he might look like or whether he had become the actor or singer or artist she had pictured him becoming. And she didn't tell her mother that the guilt was worse than ever.

Years passed and Penny became part of a church in Los Angeles. There she grew closer to God, certain that her earlier mistakes were forgiven. Eventually she met a kind businessman, someone who shared her love of God and the arts. They married and began a life of their own. But still, voices would haunt her at night. How could she give up her child? Why would she choose a career over a baby? Where was her son now? Did he hate her for the choice she'd made?

When Penny miscarried their first child, a dam broke in her soul. She wept for days, wondering if maybe God was punishing her for giving away her firstborn. Never mind what the women's minister at her church told her, that adoption was clearly the kindest option she could have chosen. She still felt like an awful mother, even after she had three children with her husband. As seventeen years passed she knew only one thing could ease that.

She would need to hear from her son himself that he was happy about the adoption. That he was doing well in the home where he'd been placed. Penny tried to look up the adoption records and find out whether it was possible to locate his adoptive parents.

But the attorney had been right. The records were absolutely confidential.

"You can write your son a letter and have it put in his file," one of the clerks at the state records department told her. "That way if he comes looking for you, he'll know your thoughts, even your address if you want him to know that."

Penny had no other choice.

That weekend she went on a retreat with her church. One of the days was set aside for reflection, time to walk along the shores of Lake Superior, thinking about God and the place each of the women was at in her journey of faith.

Penny had no interest in walking or thinking. She hovered over her hotel room desk and—with only an occasional glance at the lake—she wrote the letter to her son. First she talked about the situation that had led to her getting pregnant, about the plans she'd had and her inability to be a mother. Then she explained that she had regretted the choice ever since.

"Don't hate me, please. I did what I thought was best for you. But believe me, I won't have peace until I hear from you, until I know that you've read my apology."

Penny sent the letter, prayed that one day it would reach him, and waited.

Her son turned eighteen and then nineteen, but there was no word from him.

Please, God, Penny prayed every night, *give him a curiosity about me. Drive him to the records, Lord, so he'll know how I feel about him. Then, please . . . direct him to write to me so I'll know how he feels, too.*

Penny hoped that her son's silence was a good sign, that maybe his life had been very good, his adoptive parents kind and wonderful. If that were the case, of course he wouldn't come looking for her. But still she worried and wondered, unable to set her mind at peace.

Then, three weeks after her son's twentieth birthday, Penny received a hand-addressed letter. The return address was topped with the name Jeremy Bennett. Penny's heart rate quickened. Could it be him, the son she'd thought about and prayed about for so many years?

She tore the envelope open and a simple, one-page letter spilled out. Tears blurred her eyes from the beginning:

Dear Penny,

I am Jeremy Bennett, the son you gave up for adoption twenty years ago. After my last birthday I decided to check the court records to learn what I could about you. My parents supported this idea completely. What I found was your letter, and reading it made me know I had to write back to you.

You see, Penny, I have had a wonderful life. My parents are loving Christians who have raised me to believe in God, hard work, and family. I am an undergrad student who plans to attend medical school and become a family practice doctor one day.

I think about you and how young you were, how you didn't know what you wanted from life. If you had kept me, my experience would have been so different. Maybe I wouldn't have had the wonderful siblings I've known all my life, or maybe I wouldn't have learned about God.

Maybe I wouldn't have had the chance to excel in school the way I am excelling now.

I tell you this because I want to put your mind at ease, and because I want to thank you. Giving me up for adoption to the Bennett family was the most loving thing you could have done for me. I'd like to meet you one day to thank you in person, but from this moment on don't worry for one minute that you made a wrong choice. I will always be grateful.

In Christ's love,
Jeremy Bennett

Penny's hands shook as she lowered the letter to her lap. Then she closed her eyes and raised her face to the heavens. In that moment she had the strangest feeling, almost as if she were standing on holy ground. God had worked a miracle that day, given her the reassurance she'd been desperately seeking for nearly two decades.

A month later she met Jeremy for herself and saw in his eyes that everything he'd told her was true. Adoption had been her greatest gift to him, and now he had returned that gift with his response.

"It's a miracle, Penny, us meeting after so many years." Jeremy stood back, grinning.

Penny could only nod through her tears, imagining the miracle God had given her: replacing a lifetime of guilt and doubt with a peace that would last for all time.

And God gave her something else.

An hour-long concert, compliments of her son, the medical student with an uncanny love for the arts.

CHAPTER EIGHT

◆

A Series of Miracles

When Vince Anderson was a high school sophomore, he told his sweetheart, Sharon, that he knew how life would go for them.

"I'm going to marry you one day, Sharon, and we'll have six kids."

Sharon giggled, touched by the certainty in Vince's tone. They had known each other since junior high and she didn't doubt Vince's intentions.

"Six is perfect," she told him. "Three girls and three boys."

Through high school, rough times came. Neither of them wanted a serious relationship when they were so young. Occasionally Sharon would attend a dance or see a movie with an upperclassman, and Vince would feel his heart had been torn out. Other times Sharon would enter the lunchroom in time to see another girl hanging on Vince's arm.

Finally it was their senior year and time for the biggest event of the spring calendar—the prom. From the time they were very young, they had planned to attend the senior prom together, but a month before the dance, Vince began chumming around with a brunette from his math class. When she asked him to be her date, he couldn't tell her no.

At the same time, Sharon had been receiving attention from one of the drummers in the band. The moment she knew about Vince's decision, she told the drummer she didn't have a date for the prom.

"Then you'll go with me," he told her.

And with that, the plans were made.

———

The day of the big dance came and Sharon and Vince weren't speaking to each other. Never mind that they were both silently hurt by the other's actions, neither intended to make the first move. Especially not at the dance.

But an hour into the event, they were both on the dance floor with their dates when their eyes met. Sharon was the first to look away, ashamed that her heart was fluttering because of Vince. He, too, looked away, intent on avoiding Sharon the rest of the night.

Another hour passed and Sharon had to use the restroom. She made certain Vince was with his date so there would be no chance meeting in the hall. Then she explained to the drummer that she'd be right back. Ten minutes later, on the way out of the restroom, Vince stepped out in front of her and took her hands in his.

"Why are we doing this to ourselves?" His voice was little more than a whisper. "I can't think of anyone but you."

Sharon could feel tears in her eyes. She swallowed hard, searching for the words. "Where can we go?"

"Outside." He looked over his shoulder. His date was talking to a group of her girlfriends. "They'll never miss us."

Vince and Sharon stole out the side door and sat side by side on the school lawn. "We're graduating soon."

"Yes." Sharon shivered and slid a little closer to Vince. "Sometimes I wonder whether we'll ever see each other again."

"I don't." Vince looked to the center of her soul. "You know why?"

Sharon could feel a smile tugging at her lips. Her heart was thawing a bit more with every passing second. "Why?"

"Because, remember?" He leaned in and kissed her on the lips. "I'm going to marry you one day and we'll have six kids."

She giggled and her heart leaped when he reached for her hand. "But what about our dates?"

"They'll be okay." He held her gaze. "But do me a favor, Sharon."

She felt herself breathing normally again and realized why. She was where she belonged. "What?"

"Don't ever let go again, okay?"

Sharon never did. She and Vince left the prom together that night and didn't look back once, not through college, and not after they married the summer before their senior year. The only time doubts found their way between them was five years later. Despite the plans they'd had for so long, they were unable to have children.

"We've done all we can do," the doctor told them one bleak January morning. "Have you considered adoption?"

Sharon and Vince never had. The plan they'd made as high school sophomores about having six kids was still the one they clung to. They went home dejected and that night Vince took her outside.

"Remember that night at the prom?" His voice was low as he put his arm around her shoulders.

"Yes." She bit her lip. "Our poor dates."

"But think about it. Only God could have brought us together at a time like that. It was something I'd prayed about and when things worked out, I felt like he'd given me the greatest answer of all."

She tilted her face toward him and let the cool winter breeze wash away her anxiety. "Yes. It was amazing, wasn't it?"

"It was." He searched her eyes. "And so it's no different now. We have to believe God has a plan in all of this. He's brought us too far to let us down now."

That night the two of them prayed for a miracle, that God would fill their house with children the way only he could do. After much discussion over the next few weeks, they made a call to a local international adoption agency. A brief education on available children convinced them of their next step.

They would adopt a little girl from China—a place where boys are the cherished children and girls often aborted because of their gender.

The process was long and arduous, but it brought Sharon and Vince even closer together. Finally they were matched with a child, a four-year-old girl named Mai Lan. Sharon and Vince flew to China and visited Mai Lan in the orphanage—immediately they fell in love with her. She had huge brown doe eyes, and a smile that played on her lips despite her shyness.

"We have one question." Vince stepped forward when they met with the director of the orphanage. "We'd like to have many children. Does Mai Lan have any siblings?"

The director shook her head. "Her brothers aren't up for adoption, and Mai Lan is the only girl. I'm sorry." He waved his hand toward the room where dozens of children played. "Certainly we have other children if you're interested."

Sharon and Vince were, but they decided to adopt only Mai Lan, and when they brought her home to their Chicago townhouse they gave her the nickname Molly. A sibling would've been wonderful, especially another little girl, but if Molly had no sisters, it must not have been meant to be.

For the next two years, Sharon and Vince savored every moment with their new daughter. She was a sponge who learned to read just after her fifth birthday. But every once in a while she would say something about Mai Lin, a girl Sharon and Vince knew nothing about.

"Is Mai Lin your friend?" Vince would ask, and Molly would shake her head, her expression earnest.

"She's my sister. My little sister."

Vince and Sharon would exchange looks then, convinced that their daughter had a vivid imagination. "Honey," Sharon would say, "you don't have a sister."

"I do, Mommy. Her name is Mai Lin."

The couple wondered if maybe Molly were making up the little girl since Mai Lin's name was so similar to her own. But though she had no specific memories she could recall, the memory of the girl she called a sister remained.

Time passed, and the idea of Molly's strange memory was quickly overshadowed by Sharon's amazing news not quite a year after Molly's adoption. Against all medical understanding, Sharon was pregnant, and nine months later she delivered healthy twin boys.

Even with the busyness of a house full of three

children, Molly still occasionally spoke of her sister. On the two-year anniversary of Molly's adoption, Sharon and Vince made the decision. If Molly wanted a sister, then they would adopt another little girl from China. Not a biological sister, but a child who would at least look like her.

An early check, though, showed that the orphanage where they'd adopted Molly was closed down. A local agency gave them information about another orphanage, one located fifty miles from the first one they'd worked with. After six months they went to China and met the little girl they'd chosen, a five-year-old named Christine.

From the beginning, Sharon and Vince were struck by the resemblance between Molly and Christine. "It's uncanny," Vince told his wife on the flight home. "They could be the same child."

Molly and Christine were fast friends from the beginning. They talked the same, laughed the same, and enjoyed playing with dolls and jumping rope.

"She's my sister, Mommy," Molly said one morning after breakfast. "Thank you for bringing me my sister."

Sharon felt uncomfortable, but she chuckled lightly. "Of course she's your sister, Molly. She's in our family just like the babies. All four of you are brothers and sisters."

But when Christine wound up allergic to wheat and dairy, the same as Molly, Sharon approached Vince. "I want the girls tested; I want their DNA checked." Sharon's hands trembled as she explained the reasons. "What if they really are sisters, Vince?"

"It's impossible. You know what the orphanage director told us. Molly had no sisters."

"I know, but what if? Molly's talked about a sister from the beginning." Sharon paused. "I couldn't go all my life without knowing."

Vince agreed, if only to put Sharon's doubts at ease. Over the next few weeks the girls visited the doctor for checkups and had their blood drawn. The couple was together when they got the news that rocked their world.

Molly and Christine were full biological sisters.

The odds were beyond anything anyone could explain, but Sharon contacted the orphanage and found out the story as best as it could be relayed.

Apparently the birth mother of the girls had three daughters. She kept her oldest and tried to hide the next two. Both times, when local government officials caught on to her ruse, her daughters were taken away.

In this case, the official changed the name of the woman's third daughter to Christine. Originally her name had been Mai Lin—the name Molly remembered as belonging to her sister.

The entire situation felt like a series of miracles to Sharon and Vince, a couple who might not have realized any of their dreams if not for a bold move the two of them made at the senior prom. It's something they talk about often, when they're not busy running their six children around.

In addition to Molly and Christine and the twin boys, Sharon gave birth to another son and finally a daughter, making the miracle of their lives complete, and Vince's promise he'd made his sophomore year right on.

CHAPTER NINE

Miracle of the Heart

Kate English lost her heart sometime after her junior year in college. Kurt, the young man she fell in love with, was perfect in every way. He was interested in criminal justice, same as her. He shared her faith and love of the outdoors. And especially because he loved children.

"We'll have a whole houseful of kids," Kurt would tell her as they strolled the campus hand in hand.

Kate felt that God had hand-delivered Kurt to her. They spent the fall of their senior year planning a summer wedding and looking forward to the future.

But a few months later, Kate and Kurt were driving across Pennsylvania to see her parents when they were hit head-on by a drunk driver. Kurt broke his leg but survived the accident with no permanent injuries.

Not so for Kate.

Her face broke the windshield, and she landed on the pavement ten yards away. She was left with a crushed pelvis, internal injuries, and a jagged scar across her right cheek. The news came soon afterward that because of the damage to her pelvic area, she would never be able to have children. She was still in the hospital when Kurt visited one afternoon and poured out his feelings.

"I don't know how to say this." He looked at his hands. Kate noticed a thin layer of perspiration on his upper lip.

Kate winced against the pain in her midsection

and sat up straighter. Her heartbeat felt strangely irregular as she studied Kurt's face. "What is it?"

A long sigh came from Kurt's lips. "I'm having . . ." His eyes lifted and met hers. "I'm having second thoughts about getting married."

For several seconds, Kate stared at him, mouth open. Then the room began to tilt and she closed her eyes to keep from feeling dizzy. Nothing had changed between them. Why now, three weeks after the accident, would Kurt be having doubts? When she opened her eyes, she saw something in his eyes that hadn't been there before.

A strange coolness and an unyielding certainty.

She massaged her throat and struggled to find her voice. "Are you . . . are you confused? I mean, everything's crazy right now, but we'll get through it, won't we?" There was panic in her voice. A panic she hated. "Or maybe it was something I did, something we can talk about?"

A dozen possibilities crossed her mind in that moment. But not for a minute did Kate expect what came out of Kurt's mouth next.

"I want children, Kate." Anguish filled his voice.

"It's the reason I want to get married—so that I can have a family."

His words hit her like so many flaming arrows. "I see." Her words were barely a whisper, her heart breaking in half. "I can't have kids, so you don't want to marry me, is that it?"

Kurt took her hand; his palms were sweaty. "I'm sorry. I know it sounds terrible, but I can't change the way I feel." He crossed his arms and took a step back from Kate's hospital bed. "Everything's different now." He apologized again and told her good-bye.

It was the last time Kate ever saw him.

The fallout was devastating. Kate couldn't decide which Kurt had run away from—the fact that she couldn't have children, or that her face was disfigured. She spent two months in the hospital and then went home to complete her rehabilitation. Every day she fell deeper into a depression that knew no bounds.

Her parents were furious with Kurt, willing to do anything to help Kate rebound. But the news was too devastating. In a period of eight weeks she had lost everything that mattered. Her fiancé, her good looks, and her ability to have children.

Even her faith.

"God allowed this," she would tell her mother. "No one will want me now."

"Kurt was wrong in what he did," her mother would insist. "God will have someone else for you one day. You'll see."

But Kate's depression grew worse, until she had no interest in getting out of bed—even after her injuries were healed. The questions assaulted her constantly. How could Kurt have left her? Was it really that easy to walk away from someone you'd planned to marry? And what would her life be like now, her face scarred, her body forever barren?

Alone in the darkness each night, Kate had no answers for herself.

Finally, her parents insisted on counseling. The sessions ran three times a week, and over the course of the year Kate felt herself changing. What had been a deep and desperate sorrow became a steely determination. She wouldn't roll over and die because a drunk driver had ruined her life. Kurt was gone and he wasn't coming back. She wouldn't lie in bed dreading the past, not any longer.

The next year Kate finished college and earned her Emergency Medical Technician certificate at the same time. Gradually her faith returned, and she found great peace in her relationship with God. No matter if Kurt had left, no matter how many people stared at her face with pity in their eyes, God would be there for her. He hadn't allowed the car accident. Drunk drivers were part of a fallen world.

And she couldn't navigate a fallen world without God.

At the end of that year, Kate was sure about what she wanted to do with her life, and she sought after it with a passion. If a car accident could change someone's life the way this one had changed hers, then she would become a paramedic.

The job turned out to be everything Kate hoped it would be. The combination of prayer and all she'd learned through training gave her the chance to administer not only emergency assistance, but hope and peace to the victims she came across.

_____

Only one area of struggle remained in Kate's life. She still had trouble connecting with men. Occasionally she would stay after work talking with another paramedic or one of the firefighters who worked the same areas as she did. But always she felt them looking at her, not into her.

"They don't see who I am on the inside," Kate told her mother. "They see someone with a scar across her face."

Kate could only imagine what they would think if they knew the rest of the story. That she couldn't have children. And so she kept walls up around her heart, never allowing herself more than a brief, shallow conversation with the men in her life. All the while two desires burned in her heart and over time they became prayers—prayers for not one, but two miracles.

"Please, God," she would pray when she was alone at night, "please help me learn to love. Bring someone into my life who will accept me the way I am. And please let me care for a child one day."

Months became years and still Kate struggled to let down the walls around her heart. Her lonely place in life was at least in part her own fault, but she felt helpless to move beyond her fears, to let down her guard and risk having what happened with Kurt happen again. Finally, on the morning of Kate's twenty-seventh birthday she uttered a desperate prayer.

"God, I give you my whole life. If you don't want me to find love, if children aren't in my future, so be it. I'll keep working as a paramedic, helping people the best I know how. I give it all over to you."

That day Kate felt more free than she'd felt in years. Instead of feeling sorry for herself, desperate for a miraculous change, she embraced the reality of her life. One of her coworkers, a single paramedic named Tom, commented on the difference.

"You're glowing today, Kate." He patted her back. The two of them had known each other for three years, but Kate had never allowed anything close to a deep conversation with him. Now he smiled, his eyes meeting hers. "Let me take you out for coffee after work. It's your birthday, after all."

Kate fought the instinct to shut out the offer, to assume he was feeling sorry for her. Instead she smiled and agreed. Coffee with this man would be enjoyable; God would take care of her insecurities.

But before the shift ended, an emergency call came in. There had been a fatal traffic accident on the freeway, not two miles from the station. Kate and Tom were two of the first emergency personnel on the scene. What they saw was heartbreaking. The victims' car had gone off the freeway and rolled into a ravine. No other cars were involved, so police assumed immediately that the driver was under the influence of either drugs or alcohol, or he'd fallen asleep at the wheel.

By the looks of it, two people were trapped inside the car, a man and a woman. Both appeared to be dead. Special machinery was needed to get to the bodies inside the car, and only halfway through the procedure did they hear the small, stifled cries of a child coming from the backseat.

"There's someone alive inside!" Kate had been standing nearby, waiting to give emergency care to the victims if either of them could be helped.

Now that they were certain there was at least one living victim, Kate and Tom made their way past the workers to what remained of the mangled vehicle. Strapped in the backseat were not one, but two children—an infant in a car seat, eyes wide open and alert. And a boy, maybe two or three years old, in an upright car seat. He was crying, his head bleeding, his eyes filled with terror.

In fifteen minutes, working alongside the emergency crews, Kate and Tom were able to get the children out of the vehicle. As they worked they were both aware of a heavy smell of alcohol. Once the children were out, Kate stayed with them, taking their vital signs, making sure they had no serious injuries.

The boy had huge brown eyes and olive-colored skin. He held tight to Kate's hand, looking at her every few seconds. "Mommy?"

"It's okay, honey." Kate tried to smile, her voice shaking. "What's your name?"

The boy didn't answer the question. Instead he reached out, took hold of his little sister's hand, and cuddled close to Kate. Occasionally he would raise one hand, his palm turned upward. "Mommy, bye-bye?"

By the time Tom had helped to remove the bodies of the two adults, Kate felt a bond with the little boy and his infant sister that went beyond explanation. Tom motioned for her to follow him a few feet away. Kate left another paramedic in charge of the children.

"Police have the details." Tom's face was grim. "The children's mother is in jail; she signed her rights to her only living relative—her sister. The deceased couple is the sister and her husband. Apparently the male victim has a history of drunk driving arrests. If the crash hadn't killed them, alcohol poisoning might have. They reek of alcohol still."

Kate looked back at the children. "Who'll care for the kids now?"

"Social services." Tom bit his lip. "They'll take the kids to the hospital to be checked. By tonight they'll become part of the system, two more kids waiting for a home."

A lump formed in Kate's throat. "The boy is . . . he's very special." Her voice was soft, strained. "We've been talking."

Something gentle flashed in Tom's eyes. "I was watching. Looks like you made yourself a little friend."

The boy's name was Peter, and his sister was Cassie. Tom was right about how things played out over the next two days. The children were checked at the hospital and found to have only surface scratches and bruises. Then they were placed with social services and put in a temporary foster home.

Kate couldn't get the little boy out of her head. The feel of his little hand in hers was something that stayed with her no matter how many hours and days passed. A week after the accident, Kate had a dream. In it, she saw herself with little Peter and Cassie, caring for them. Parenting them.

The next morning she went to work and talked to Tom. "I'm thinking of taking them in, seeing if I could get emergency approval to foster them, maybe even adopt them one day."

Tom's eyes sparkled, the corners of his lips lifting in approval. "Let me know if it works out. I'll do whatever I can to help."

Kate made the calls and things came together

faster than she could have imagined. Because of her job working with the county, many of the checks on her background had already been done. Four weeks after the accident, Peter and Cassie were placed in her home as long-term foster kids.

When she was at work, Kate's mother and father watched the children, and from the beginning Kate knew they were an answer to prayer in her life. "The miracle I've been waiting for," she told her parents.

Tom made good on his word. He came around several times a week when he and Kate were off work. Sometimes he'd stay and talk to Kate, opening up to her about his past and his own accomplishments, dreams, and losses. Other times he would sit on the floor and play with Peter, or rock Cassie when she was tired and couldn't be comforted.

What started as a friendship of common likes and experiences soon became more. Tom told Kate he was falling in love with her, and Kate fought her desire to shut him out, to refuse his affection on grounds that he would certainly walk out of her life one day as Kurt had.

Meanwhile, the children were very healthy despite their rocky beginning. Neither of them had obvious physical or emotional handicaps, and they took to Kate as if she'd been their mother forever.

"I can feel God working in my life," she told Tom one night after the kids were asleep. "Just when I'd given up hope, he's bringing about a miracle right before my eyes."

The next step took place six months later when Kate got approval to officially adopt the children. That night, Tom came to celebrate with her. When the children were asleep, he pulled out a ring and asked her the question she never expected to hear again. "Will you marry me, Kate? Let me be a father to Peter and Cassie, let me love you all the days of my life?"

Questions rose in Kate's heart. What about her face? What about the children she couldn't have? But she and Tom had talked about those issues, and he didn't care. In what felt like a second miracle,

Tom truly loved her for who she was—regardless of everything.

Tears filled her eyes as Kate took the ring, kissed Tom, and told him yes. They were married on her twenty-eighth birthday, and Kate marveled at the turns her life had taken. One car accident had shut the door on her future, ending her chances at love with Kurt and at being a mother to her own biological children.

But the other had brought about not one, but two miracles. Two months after their wedding, Kate and Tom stood hand in hand, overcome with emotion as a judge finalized their adoption of Peter and Cassie. This time when Peter looked up at her and said, "Mommy?" Kate smiled back and took his hand.

"I'm here, honey. And I'll always be here."

CHAPTER TEN

An Angel in Disguise

Jared Winters loved Allison Hayes from the moment he saw her late one August afternoon the summer before his freshman year. Allison was walking with three girlfriends around the track at Washington High School outside Fairfax, Virginia, and for no reason in particular she looked up.

The football team was holding twice-daily practices that week, and Jared was hot, sweaty, and exhausted. Even still, from his place in the middle of the pack, his eyes met hers and for a moment it seemed they were the only two on the field. She was tall with long legs, pale blonde hair, and brown eyes that stood out from fifty yards away. Jared had never seen a more beautiful girl in all his life.

"What you staring at, Winters?" His buddy was stretching out next to him.

"Her." Jared maintained eye contact with the girl. "She's gorgeous."

His friend followed Jared's gaze and chuckled. "That's Allison Hayes."

Jared felt his heart leap. He looked at his buddy. "You know her."

"She lives down the street from me." He gave a sideways nod of his head. "She's one of the untouchables. Every guy who sees her remembers her."

Jared found out as much information as he could. Allison was a freshman who had attended the middle school across town. She ran track and paid little attention to the boys who sought after her. Before practice was over, Jared found his buddy again. "You heard it from me first. One day Allison's going to be my girl."

His friend only laughed and gave Jared an easy shove in the shoulder. "Yeah, and I'll be president of the United States."

School started two weeks later and Jared uttered one prayer throughout the day—*please, God, let me see her.*

The answer came in sixth period. After an entire day of wondering whether or not she had actually enrolled at Washington High, Allison Hayes walked in five minutes late to Jared's American history class. Her seat was completely across the room, but throughout the hour Jared never took his eyes off her.

Not once did she look his way, but when the bell rang she hesitated near the door. As Jared walked past she lifted her face and looked at him. "Hi." Her smile lit up his heart.

"Hi." He nodded, falling in next to her as they left the classroom. "I'm Jared."

"Freshmen football, right?"

"Yeah." Jared could barely feel his feet against the hallway floor. She knew who he was! He drew in a deep breath. He wasn't dreaming. Allison Hayes was really walking beside him, smiling at him. "You run track, right?"

A light blush filled her cheeks. "Not till spring, but yes. I'm a sprinter."

The conversation continued as they headed for their next classes, and picked up again every day that week after sixth period. Finally, at the end of the second week, Jared asked for her phone number. That night he told his mother about the beautiful blonde from his history class.

"If she'll go out with me, I really think we'll be together forever." Jared sat down across from her at the kitchen table. "Could that happen, Mom? Do you think it could?"

His mother was writing a letter. She set her pen down and looked up at Jared. "Once in a while you meet someone very special." She raised an eyebrow, her eyes dancing. "Even when you're technically too young to date."

Jared laughed. "We wouldn't really go anywhere, Mom. You know that."

She grinned at him. "You got that right." She hesitated, her smile warmer than before. "But I'm glad you think she's special."

Through phone calls and study sessions at his house, Jared and Allison grew close. By the time they were sophomores, everyone at Washington knew they were an item.

"Man, don't you wanna sample the wares?" one of his football friends asked him at the start of his junior year. "Allison's great and all, but look at other options."

Jared only smiled and shook his head. There were no other options. Allison was the girl of his dreams, and the truth became truer all the time. Their relationship carried over from high school to the campus of Pepperdine University in Malibu, California, and for the first time they had to take a long look at their physical relationship.

Both Jared and Allison had been active in their church youth groups through high school, and though they'd kissed, they had agreed to not let their relationship get more physical. But after traveling across the country to attend the same private university, the temptations were greater, the opportunities to compromise far more frequent.

One night they took a walk along a campus hillside overlooking the Pacific Ocean, and Jared opened the discussion. He talked about how they had plans to stay pure and how things had changed. "If we don't make a decision here, I'm not sure either one of us will hold to our intentions."

Allison's expression was serious. "You're right. What should we do?"

Jared swallowed hard. "Let's make a promise, before God. If we do, I really believe he'll bless us no matter how things wind up between us."

Then and there, Jared and Allison held hands and lifted their faces toward the blue California sky. "God, we promise to stay pure for you, to do things your way." He hesitated, his heart beating hard. "Help us keep our promise. And please bless our relationship."

The blessings seemed to pour out.

Jared and Allison found new ways to socialize in groups, and the commitment they made to stay pure became attainable. In addition, they did well in their schoolwork and the summer before their junior year, Jared took Allison to dinner at a restaurant on Malibu Beach and proposed to her.

Allison said yes, and the plans were set in motion. The wedding would be a year later. They began dreaming about a wedding the summer before their senior year in college.

"How many kids do you want when you're older?" Jared was sharing a picnic with her. It was two months before their wedding, and they'd both found jobs in Los Angeles. Jared had purchased a condo in Thousand Oaks, where the couple would live after they were married.

Allison leaned back and looked at a trail of distant clouds. "I don't know." She shrugged and found his eyes again. "Two at least, don't you think?"

"However many it takes to get a little girl who looks like you—blonde hair and brown eyes." He grinned at her. "Even if she's our tenth child, that's what I want."

The wedding was everything Jared and Allison dreamed it would be. Before the reception was over, Jared's mother slipped over and whispered in Allison's ear: "Now you can give me those grandbabies I've been wanting!"

Allison could feel herself blush. "Give us a while, Mom." She patted her mother-in-law. "We haven't had our honeymoon yet."

But the truth was, she and Jared both wanted children sooner rather than later. The more they talked about the idea of a family, the more certain they were that they wanted several children.

On their one-year anniversary, they put away all forms of birth control and began praying for children. The year passed slowly, and each month Allison would go to Jared with the disappointing news. No babies yet. By their next anniversary, Allison worried constantly that something must be wrong.

"Let's get checked out." Jared ran his hand soothingly along the back of her head, pulling her close. "Maybe it's something the doctor can help us with."

The problem turned out to be with Allison. She had trouble ovulating, and most of her eggs were not fully developed.

"I could put you on fertilization drugs," the doctor told her. "But I'd still tell you the odds of your getting pregnant are slim to none."

Allison wept in Jared's arms that night. "What should we do?" She looked up, her eyes filled with hopelessness. "God knows we want children."

Jared thought about the little girl he'd dreamed of having, the one who would look just like Allison. He swallowed hard. "Let's try the medication. It's worth a go. If it doesn't work, we'll decide then what to do next."

The medication was hard on Allison, causing headaches and other side effects. But she didn't mind any of it, as long as she had a chance at getting pregnant. It wasn't until another year passed and the couple was about to celebrate their third anniversary that they agreed to stop the medication.

For weeks they grieved the loss of the children they would never know. Then they committed the issue to prayer and came to the same conclusion. It was time to look at the other possibility—adoption.

After much research, Jared and Allison decided against domestic adoption. "It's too risky," Allison told her mother that week. "I couldn't stand the idea of adopting a child and having a birth mother change her mind."

Jared agreed, and they contacted the One Family International Adoption Agency in Los Angeles. After meeting with a counselor and going through a home study, Allison and Jared agreed to adopt a child from Russia.

When it came time to specify what sort of child they would be interested in adopting, Jared hesitated. Privately he shared his heart on the matter with Allison. "I want to ask for a blonde, brown-eyed little girl." He searched Allison's eyes. "But I don't think that's what God wants us to ask for. Somewhere out there he has a perfect child, just for us." He hesitated. "I guess I don't want to limit him."

Allison felt her heart swell. Jared had dreamed of having a daughter like that for so long. She loved the fact that he was willing to give up on his dream, all so that the right child might be placed in their home. She took his hands and gently squeezed his fingers. "I feel the same way."

And so they filled out the forms with open-ended answers. Any child, any sex, any hair color would be fine for them.

Six months later they were called into the adoption agency office and told that a baby was available. It was a boy, six months old, brown hair, brown eyes, with a foot that was slightly mis-shapen. She went on to explain that most of the babies at that particular orphanage had dark hair and eyes, a look common to that region of Russia.

The social worker sounded concerned as she presented the details. "Is that going to be a problem for you? The fact that the baby might have some health issues?"

Allison looked down and saw that her hands

were trembling. Next to her, Jared clenched his jaw and gave a slight nod. They had prayed about this child, refusing to limit God as to which type of baby he placed in their arms. Now there was a knowing that the two of them felt exactly the same way.

Jared cleared his throat and looked at the social worker. "If that's the baby you found for us, then that's our son."

Eight weeks later, the couple boarded a plane and set off for Russia. They had a photograph of their new son, and a courage that could have come only from God. The next day they showed up for their appointment at the Russian orphanage.

"We are excited that you will adopt little Ina." The woman smiled. "She seems just right for you."

Allison and Jared exchanged a frown and then looked at the woman again. Allison spoke first. "I'm afraid there's been a mix-up of some kind." She felt the corners of her lips rise a bit as she set the photograph on the desk between them. "This is the baby we're here to adopt. His name is Ramon."

The woman took the photo, stared at it, and shook her head. "Ramon was a very sick baby, ma'am." She bit her lip and handed the photo back to Allison. "He was placed with a local family, a couple who takes sick children and sees to their medical needs."

"But all along, we were told he was our baby. Now you're saying you have a little girl for us?" Jared's heart beat hard beneath his shirt. They were prepared for a baby boy with a deformed foot. If the orphanage had a girl for them, how old was she? And what might be wrong with her?

"Yes." The orphanage worker smiled at Allison and Jared. "Ina is six months old, also. She's a beautiful little girl."

She would have dark hair and eyes, the same as the other children at the orphanage. But Allison was afraid to ask the next question: "What physical issues does Ina have, ma'am?"

The woman checked the chart and gave a slow shake of her head. "Ina was brought to us just a week ago. Her parents died in an accident." She looked up at Allison and Jared. "From everything we know about Ina, she's in perfect health."

The change was enough to make Allison's head spin. The boy they'd been praying for had been placed with someone else? Now a daughter was waiting for them? Beside her, Jared squeezed her hand and Allison saw the determination in his eyes. Their determination remained the same. Whatever baby God had planned for them would be theirs. No question.

Allison took Jared's hand. "Well, then"—she gave the woman a tentative smile—"could we meet her?"

A grin broke out on the woman's face. "I'll be right back."

While the woman was gone, Jared looked at her. "Remember that picnic back before we were married? When we talked about having a houseful of kids?"

"I remember." Warmth spread across Allison's heart. "I guess this is the beginning of the journey."

Jared said nothing about his blonde, brown-eyed

little girl, the one they would probably never have now. They were committed to whatever future God had for them, and whatever children God placed in their lives.

At that moment, the woman came around the corner, carrying a baby bundled in a faded pink blanket. As soon as they could see her face, Allison's breath caught in her throat. Next to her, she felt Jared react the same way.

"She's beautiful." Jared took a step closer, holding out his arms as the woman passed Ina over.

Allison pulled the blanket down and took a closer look. Jared was right; their new little daughter was absolutely perfect. But it was more than that. Ina had pale blonde hair and brown eyes. "She looks . . ." Jared's voice caught as he turned and stared at Allison. "She looks just like you."

The orphanage worker smiled. "Yes, many of our babies have light hair at first. But I would guess Ina's hair will be dark when she's older. Probably by the time she turns two."

The woman's opinion didn't matter. Jared and Allison were delighted with their little daughter.

A week later they went home and started their life together. But the biggest surprise came that fall when Allison found out the amazing truth—she was pregnant.

"This happens sometimes," the doctor told her. "A woman will try and try to have a baby. Then after an adoption goes through, she winds up pregnant." He grinned. "I always figure it was God's plan, somehow."

In fact, Allison and Jared went on to have four healthy, dark-haired little boys. To this day, only one of their children has Allison's pale blonde hair and brown eyes—their oldest child, Ina.

A child who came from nowhere, a gift of God and a reminder to Allison and Jared that their dreams matter. And that long ago at a sunny afternoon picnic, all of heaven heard the desires of their hearts and set about seeing them take place.

CHAPTER ELEVEN

Second Chances

Christopher Owens studied the packed camp building and the faces looking back at him. They were foster kids, all of them. Children abandoned or neglected or taken away from their parents. Their week at Second Chances Summer Camp each July was probably the highlight of the year for most of them.

Christopher fought back memories as he looked from one child to another and drew a deep breath.

"My message for you is simple." He took a few steps closer to the edge of the stage. "God has a plan for your life. No matter how it feels right now, God has a plan."

Then, as he did every year at this time, he allowed himself to go back. Back twenty-two years to the summer when he was just six years old. He had been an only child, the son of a drug-dealer father and an alcoholic mother. The shady dealings of his parents and the strange people who came and went through his house back then had seemed like a normal life.

Yes, once in a while he would watch his father push his mother around, slap her in the face or shove her to the ground. And sometimes he would hear his parents talking about him.

"We gotta get rid of the kid, Emma. You know it as well as I do."

His mother talked funny, her words slurred and her eyes half shut. "I don't wanna get rid of him. He's fine on his own."

Sometimes his mother would pull him onto her lap and rock him. She must have been crying, because his hair would get wet on top. "I'm sorry,

Christopher. I've told Jesus I'm sorry. This isn't any kind of life for a little boy." She would shake a little. "God forgive me . . . forgive me."

His parents' words almost always frightened Christopher, but not nearly as much as what happened that Christmas. Things got out of hand between his parents, at least that's what his social worker told him later. His father fired a gun at a mean guy who stopped by the house. And somehow his mother got in the way of the bullets. She fell down a few feet from Christopher and never got up again.

"Mommy!" Christopher could still hear his little boy cry, still feel the way the words felt in his heart and on his lips that day. "Mommy, wake up! Please, Mommy!"

The whole time, his daddy sat at the table with his head in his hands, crying and mumbling something about his life being over. But his mother didn't blink or talk or do anything but lie there.

In a few minutes police officers came running through the door, and after that an ambulance pulled up outside his house. It was the last time

Christopher saw either of his parents. The social worker explained the situation to him that night after he was taken to a big house on the other side of town. His mommy was dead, gone to be with Jesus. His father, on the other hand, had gone to jail to be with the other bad guys.

And Christopher would stay with the nice family in the big house. At least for now, until the social services department could find someone to care for Christopher forever, to adopt him and make him their very own.

Christopher would never forget the way he felt that spring. The Owens family was wonderful, kind and good and safe. But Christopher didn't dare hope the family might one day be his own. His social worker told him from the beginning that the situation was only temporary, until something permanent could be worked out with someone else—his forever family.

That summer, the Owenses sent him to the Second Chance Summer Camp in Kansas City, Missouri, an hour from the house where the Owenses lived. By then, Christopher was desperately afraid and lonely. He wanted his mother in the worst way. Things had been bad back then, but at least he'd had a family, a home to call his own.

"Christopher," Mrs. Owens told him before he went to camp, "God has a plan for your life. While you're at camp, pray that God will make that plan clear to all of us, okay?"

She and Mr. Owens hugged him, as did the Owenses' two older daughters. It was at camp that Christopher learned the message of God's love and his second chances for all people. For the first time in his life, Christopher wasn't afraid or lonely or anxious about the future. Jesus—the one the camp counselors talked about—was on his side, looking out for him, walking beside him. Maybe everything would be all right, after all.

Before he left, he went to the front of the camp meeting center and got down on his knees. The counselor had told them to ask Jesus for the best dreams in their hearts. He gulped twice and began the most important prayer he'd ever prayed. "Please, God, let the Owens family be my forever family. Please."

When Christopher came home, he knew right away that something strange was going on. Balloons filled the front yard and ribbons were strung between the trees. On the house was a banner, and Mrs. Owens read it out loud for him. "Welcome to your forever home, Christopher!"

Christopher looked from Mrs. Owens to Mr. Owens, his little heart racing within him. "What . . . what does it mean?"

"We've been trying to adopt you." Mr. Owens put his arm around Christopher's shoulders. "But we couldn't put the paperwork through until the courts gave us the okay."

Christopher held his breath, afraid if he blinked he might wake up and find he'd only been dreaming.

"While you were gone, the paperwork came through." Mrs. Owens kissed him on the forehead. "Would you like to be our son forever, Christopher?"

He wanted to talk. He wanted to open his mouth and shout to the heavens, "Yes!" Yes, he wanted to be their son and live with them as part of their family forever more! Yes, of course. But tears blurred his eyes and a thick feeling made the words stick in his throat. His heart was happier than it had ever been, even if the words wouldn't come. And so he threw his arms around Mrs. Owens's neck, and then Mr. Owens's neck, and held on even as they walked inside.

From that day on, Christopher's life was different, changed. His faith in God grew, and there seemed to be truth in everything the counselor at the Second Chances camp had said. Jesus did hear his prayers; he did care about a lost little boy who didn't have a home or a hope in the world.

The years found Christopher growing in the grace of God with every year. He was always top of his class, an athlete with a kind, compassionate heart and a love for his family that went beyond that of most boys his age. As he set off for college, his adopted parents told him he could become whatever he dreamed of becoming. A doctor, a lawyer, a teacher, a coach, even a preacher.

But Christopher's goal never wavered once through college. He was hired a few months after his graduation to be a counselor at the Second Chance Summer Camp in Missouri. Today, Christopher runs the camp and every summer he shares with hopeless, lonely little boys the same message someone once shared with him.

Tears choked his voice, but his words were strong as he finished his talk that afternoon. "And so believe it, boys, believe it more than you've ever believed anything in your life. God has a plan for you, a good plan to give you a hope and a future. The same way he had a plan for me."

CHAPTER TWELVE

❧

Our Adoption Miracle

(Note: Many of you may know that Karen and her husband, Don, have adopted three little boys from Haiti. The following is an account of their own miracle story, the one that details the footprints of God in their lives.)

Like many couples, after the birth of our second child, my husband, Don, and I figured we were finished having children. But when I got pregnant with Austin five years later, the idea was out on the table again. Because of the age gap between

Kelsey and Tyler, our oldest two, and our newest little addition to the family, we considered having more children.

But when Austin was three weeks old, he was diagnosed with a deadly heart defect. He had emergency surgery and barely survived. His survival was, in itself, a miracle. The doctor was clear about our future: If you have more children, the odds are very high that they will have the same heart defect.

We spent much time in prayer and decided that we were finished having biological children, and that God just might be leading us toward adoption. For two years we put the subject on hold, raising Austin and seeing to his decreasing medical needs.

On his second birthday, we took stock of our lives and thanked God for the continued good health of all our children. Somehow we felt God was still calling us to parent more children, and with Austin healthier than ever, we began to explore the possibilities.

For nearly a year we looked into domestic adoption.

Our thought was that we'd adopt a little boy a year or so older than Austin and a few years younger than Tyler. That way we could keep the birth order of our children the same—Kelsey, the oldest; Tyler, the oldest son; Austin, the youngest son. We learned from research that there are thousands of U.S. kids needing homes. But as we explored the possibilities with our social worker, we learned something else. Nearly all of them have emotional, sexual, or physical abuse issues.

"By the time parental rights are severed, most children have undergone quite a bit of abuse," our social worker told us. "You could do such an adoption when your children are older. But not with a little one in the house."

Once in a while we would find a child who hadn't been abused. Neglected, yes, but not abused. But in that case, there would be a hundred home-study files ahead of ours in line for that child. As the months wore on, we became discouraged.

Maybe God wasn't calling us to adopt, after all. But about that time, a friend asked if we'd considered international adoption. We explained that we hadn't, and the friend went on to say that we should look at Haiti.

"People simply are not lined up to adopt children from Haiti," the woman told us. "Go online and check out their Web site."

We did that, and we sent away for a video about the children. The day it came, Don and I watched it after the children were in bed. On the video we saw beautiful girls and boys laughing and singing and praising God, arms outstretched. These were not the quiet, austere children typical of European orphanages. Rather they were affectionate and happy, believing with all their hearts that the prayers they uttered—prayers for families—would one day be answered.

When the video was over, Don looked at me and there was the hint of tears in his eyes. "Well"—he grinned at me—"looks like we need a bigger house."

Indeed.

About a week later, late one night alone in my office, I met EJ.

In the quiet, incandescent glow of my computer screen, I discovered an Internet site with a photo-listing of children available for adoption in Haiti. One of those was a darling five-year-old boy with huge brown eyes and a dimpled smile. "EJ is a charmer," the accompanying description said. "He's the first to hug the workers at the orphanage each day and is easily one of the fastest learners in our classroom."

To my surprise, I instantly felt a connection to EJ. In a moment's time, Haiti no longer was another country with starving, homeless children; rather, it was the homeland of this precious child. I could almost hear him calling out to us: "Mommy, Daddy . . . I love you. Please come take me home. I need a family. Please . . ."

Up until this point, any family discussion on adoption had been brief and general. We were busy, after all—my husband, Don, with teaching and coaching; me, with my writing. Besides, we already had three beautiful children. Even though adoption had crossed our minds, even after our

domestic search, we still weren't completely convinced this was the direction God was leading us.

All that changed the moment I found EJ.

I called Don into my office and for the next
hour we talked about the possibility of adopting
this sweet child. There were no disagreements. EJ
belonged in our family. Now we needed to present
the idea to our children.

From the beginning we had included our children in discussions on the idea of adopting. It
would be a family decision or none at all. Every
time we spoke about the idea, our kids were in
favor—otherwise I'm certain we wouldn't have
moved ahead. They even knew we were looking at
adopting a Haitian child. But they didn't know
about EJ.

I printed EJ's photo and the next morning Don
and I introduced him to Kelsey, Tyler, and Austin.
Setting his picture up in front of an empty chair, I
asked our kids, "How would you like EJ to be your
brother? He's five years old, and he lives in Haiti."

"Well," our only daughter, Kelsey, twelve at the

time, said as she looked at his picture thoughtfully. "He has a friendly look."

"He's five?" our seven-year-old Tyler chimed in. "That's right between me and Austin."

Two-year-old Austin just grinned and pointed. "That my brother? Huh, Mommy and Daddy? That my new brother?"

We studied EJ's picture for days. At night we prayed about him, building a bond that grew stronger with each glance at his face. He was living at the Heart of God Ministries orphanage in Port-au-Prince, so we contacted workers there about him. Finally, with full hearts, we made our decision to pursue adopting EJ.

Over the next several months, we completed a daunting amount of paperwork for the Immigration and Naturalization Service as well as a Haitian dossier. Through every step we were driven by EJ's face, his eyes. In fact, it wasn't long before we were driven by another little face as well. That of a six-year-old boy named Joshua, who was at the orphanage with EJ. The photolisting said Joshua was a happy child who excelled in academics and sports. He had great leadership qualities.

"Kids, what would you think about having two new brothers?" my husband asked our three children one evening. "EJ might like a brother who's more like him—another little boy from Haiti."

Again our kids were excited about the idea. But for reasons we didn't understand at the time, workers at the orphanage stopped us from adopting Josh. "He's a very difficult boy," one of the workers told us. "Frankly, he wouldn't blend well with other children."

With uncertainty in our souls, we decided on a different boy, a six-year-old named Sean Angelo. Six months later, we got the call every adoptive parent waits for: "Your children are ready to come home."

Haiti is widely known as one of the poorest countries in the world. It's a place rife with dangers, and there were months when I considered having our new little boys escorted home by someone else. But in the end, God made it clear that while Don stayed home to care for our three children, I was to travel to Haiti to take pictures, absorb myself in their culture, and bring home a piece of their heritage—something I could share with them later.

I was taken to the orphanage and introduced to my two new sons—EJ and Sean. The boys, both dressed in their best donated clothing, offered me shy smiles as they sat on my lap. They didn't speak a word of English.

This—all of it—was what I expected.

But I didn't expect what happened next. As I sat there searching for a common bond with EJ and Sean, a little boy walked up and brushed a lock of hair off my forehead. "Hello, Mommy." His voice was clear, his English perfect. "I love you."

Then, while the noise from forty-two orphans faded away, he sang to me, "Lord, I give you my heart . . . I give you my soul. I live for you alone . . ."

My heart was snagged in a matter of seconds. "What's your name?" I asked the child.

"Joshua," he told me. "My name's Joshua."

This was the six-year-old Joshua we'd considered adopting before finding out about Sean Angelo—the child we were told might not fit into our family! An hour later, I knew the whole story. Joshua was still up for adoption. The orphanage worker we'd talked to was no longer with the orphanage. No one had any idea why he'd given us such terribly incorrect information.

The truth was, Josh was a wonderful child, outgoing and confident, brilliant in his studies, and good with the little ones at the orphanage. He and EJ and Sean were buddies—inseparable.

I called my husband that night and wept. "Joshua belongs with us . . . I can't imagine leaving him here."

My husband's answer was something I'll never forget. "Two . . . three . . . what's the difference, Karen. If you feel that strongly about him, bring him home."

Of course, in the world of international adoption, the process is never that simple. Six months after EJ and Sean came home, Joshua followed. Only then did we feel that our family was truly complete.

———

Those early days together hold dozens of memories, moments we'll never forget. The first time EJ and Sean washed their hands in warm water, they began speaking loudly in Creole, pointing to the water and jumping up and down. It wasn't difficult to figure out why they were excited: They'd never felt warm running water before.

Then there was the day our family visited the zoo. EJ, Sean, and Joshua were mesmerized by the animals, but the experience was nothing to what came next: a trip to the grocery store.

It was a starving little boy's paradise.

As their English improved, we learned more about their past. Our boys had lost parents to starvation or illness and had gone without food for days at a time. They customarily ate something called "dirt cakes" that looked like cheap pottery made from clay, dirt, and water. Village women mixed this recipe, baked it, and gave it to the children to ease the pain in their empty tummies.

Meals came only after great effort. Our boys were adept at using rocks to knock mangoes from trees or to kill wild birds. In the early months

Sean, especially, would see a bird and nearly go ballistic, pointing and motioning toward the nearest rock. His message was simple: "Please, Daddy, this is something I can do. Let dinner be on me tonight." Politely, and with a tender heart, my husband dissuaded him from killing birds.

In those first months, we helped them deal with the basic cultural adjustments—sleeping in beds instead of on the floor, using bathrooms, learning table manners. But miraculously, the boys almost never needed to be told twice about issues of obedience. They're constantly cleaning their room and remain thrilled with their new toys and beds (they share a large bedroom with Austin and sleep in two bunk beds).

"Please, Mommy, can we vacuum?" is a question I field weekly.

"Well, okay, since you've been so good this week, I guess so."

Often people comment on the blessing we are to these little boys. But we correct them every time. Over the last three years, the blessings have been all ours.

One has been watching our three biological children embrace their new brothers. This is obvious especially when the kids play together or do homework. Because of Kelsey's, Tyler's, and Austin's efforts, our new sons were easily welcomed by their classmates. Our local school even took on the Heart of God Ministries (now out of business because of government troubles in Haiti) as a service project. Two overflowing suitcases of school supplies were collected in the early months after the boys' arrival and sent to the fledgling school operated at the orphanage.

Another blessing has been realizing the depth of faith these children have. They had nothing in Haiti, not even a chance to live. But they had a deep love for Jesus, and prayed and sang throughout the day. In a culture ridden with voodoo, it was especially comforting to know a Christian orphanage in Haiti had given these children so strong a foundation. Even now, the children love singing for God, and sometimes cry during worship time at church.

"Are you sad, honey?" my husband, Don, will sometimes ask.

"No, Daddy. I'm just so happy when I think of everything Jesus has done for me."

The boys are very loving, hugging us often and telling us—at first in Creole and now in English— exactly how much they love us. The other day, Sean said, "Mommy, when I get big, I'm going to get a job and make lots of money. I'll send some to the people in Haiti and give the rest to you."

I was puzzled by this. "That's very nice, but why do you want to give me money?"

"Because . . ." His eyes glistened. "You and Daddy have given so much to me."

People ask us about the transition. "How do you bring children into your home who have nothing in common with you?" they would inquire at the beginning. "You have different skin colors, different cultural understandings, different languages— even different food preferences."

We tell them this: with much prayer.

You see, we knew going into this adoption process that we would have different colors, different countries, different cultures. But we would have the same Christ and that, we believed, was enough. It was enough at the beginning, and it remains enough now. More than enough.

A few times we've had conversations about skin color.

"Why do I have black skin and you and Daddy and Jesus have white skin?" Sean asked once during a break from playing with his brother in the backyard.

"Well," I said, "Jesus didn't have white skin. He had brown skin. God gave everyone a special color, a color he loved for that person. All skin colors are the same in value to Jesus, and they're all beautiful."

Sean thought about that for a minute. "What color skin will I have in heaven?"

"I'm not sure." I pulled him into a quick hug. "But I hope it'll be just like it is now. Because your skin is beautiful, Sean . . . and you're such a handsome boy. I wouldn't want you to look any different than you do right now."

Sean's smile stretched across his face. "Thanks,

Mom." Then he ran out of the house to join his brothers in the backyard once again. I'll never know if that was the perfect answer, but I know this: God alone will need to provide the answers as questions such as that come up.

We're aware their Haitian background one day will be important to our sons. As such, I've learned to cook Haitian beans and rice. We eat them at least once a week and marvel at the plate-fuls of food our new boys put away. To help the boys maintain their Creole, we sometimes spend the dinner hour asking them to teach us various phrases. Truthfully, they've lost most of it. But that doesn't mean they can't get it back some other time in the future. In addition, we've networked with a small Haitian-American contingency not far from our home.

More than that, though, we stress this fact: Our primary heritage is found not in our ancestors or family genealogies or birthplaces but at the cross, in Christ alone.

There's a story often told of a particularly rough storm that came up one night and left a sandy beach strewn with starfish. The next morning a child walked along the shore, stopping every few feet to pick up a starfish and fling it back to sea. An old man watched the child and finally shouted at him, "Why bother, son? There are too many starfish to make a difference!"

With that, the boy picked up another starfish and looked at it intently before heaving it out to sea. Then turning to the old man, he said, "It makes a difference to that one."

The statistics on homeless children in our world are daunting. Orphans abound and can be found on numerous Web sites both domestically and internationally. I think about Austin's heart problems, and how his ill heart and his full heart both became the miracle that led to our willingness to adopt. And I think of the mistake the orphanage worker made about Josh—how we would never have found Sean if not for that mistake.

Adoption itself is a miracle. Every case I've ever heard of involves situations like those in our story. Certainly our family has seen the starfish principle at work amid the miracles in our lives: Adoption makes a difference.

Just ask our three new sons: EJ, Sean, and Joshua.